23B

D0709892

THE VISUAL TIME TRAVELLER

THE VISUAL TIME TRAVELLER

500 YEARS OF HISTORY, ART AND SCIENCE IN 100 UNIQUE DESIGNS

ALISON HACKETT

21C
RENAISSANCE

Published by 21st Century Renaissance 2013

Text © 21st Century Renaissance, Alison Hackett
Cover, illustrations, original design and layout
© 21st Century Renaissance, Alison Hackett

The Visual Time Traveller
500 Years of History, Art & Science
in 100 Unique Designs
ISBN 978-0-9927368-0-4

The author asserts her moral right to be
identified as the author of this work.

All rights reserved. No part of this publication
may be reproduced, stored in a retrieval system
or transmitted, in any form or by any means, electronic,
mechanical, photocopying, recording or otherwise,
without the prior permission of the publisher.

Design, illustration & production:
Origin Design, 36 Wicklow St, Dublin 2

www.origin.ie

Printed in the Netherlands:
MM Artbook printing & repro

for my mother, Lesley
18 October 1926 – 5 February 1973

In the year 2000, not long after taking up my role as the Institute of Physics Representative in Ireland, I was part of the Irish delegation that attended the Physics on Stage conference being held at CERN, the European Laboratory for Particle Physics. The first of its kind, the aim of the conference was to re-inspire physics teachers and educationalists from across Europe and to share best practice.

Wandering around this treasure trove of learning resources in the exhibition space, I came across a striking collage-style poster depicting a physics timeline made by school children stretching to about four metres along the wall. The extraordinary thing was that the poster did not include just physics theories and famous physicists, but, in addition, inserted above and below the physics timeline, were hundreds of other facts drawn from general history. Not only was this display teaching me physics but it was also giving the broadest and most interesting of contexts for that journey of learning.

From this germ, the concept for a *Physics in Time* poster was established, but not fully realised until twelve years later, by the Institute of Physics in Ireland in association with the Royal Dublin Society. Significant physics discoveries since the 16th Century were presented in a timeline along with major milestones from the worlds of exploration, art, history, politics, sport and science and displayed in a striking poster. In classrooms across the length and breadth of Ireland this poster is on display – the ultimate cross-curricular resource for any school.

My desire to develop this fascinating project further culminated in the summer of 2012 when I decided to leave the Institute of Physics to research, write and create a follow on to the poster - The Visual Time Traveller: a graphically curated narrative of history, art and science since the Renaissance.

With such a plethora of information available, the book needed a couple of structural rules. Firstly, a maximum of twelve facts would be included on any list. Only the surface could be skimmed, yet it would provide a trail of stepping-stones from which readers could take off on their own historical journeys. Secondly, the design to go with each list would be developed with a fresh concept and typography, providing a platform for innovative design to drive the narrative of historic facts.

Philosophical thoughts often hovered while I was compiling the longer lists for the book. What is history? Is it the truth? The truth is a complex thing, hard to pin down. Birth dates are known, we know when papers were published and who was victorious in which battle but we don't always know how conclusions were made or whether credit was simply being taken by those with the savviest PR skills of the day or by the documentary proof of being the first to get into print. Pertinent examples include the calculus controversy between Newton and Leibnitz and the airbrushing of Robert Hooke's image out of history - no paintings of Hooke's likeness have survived. The firm ground of historical fact can easily turn into a quicksand of doubt.

While researching, the urge to mine deeper was always present and often imperative. Seeking earlier sources of information, spiking off on tangents and adding to an exploding and chaotic file called 'more information' became the norm. An initial bald fact would flower into a resonant nuanced story and I had a growing conviction that there are very few original ideas out there – so many echo back to classical times. Themes and ideas reverberate through the ages, tapping on our shoulders lest we forget how often the past becomes our present.

The opening and closing pages of this book are marked by two powerful inventions that have profoundly influenced our ability to communicate and share information - the Gutenberg Printing Press and the World Wide Web. Printing was the main way to disseminate ideas in the sixteenth century so it is apposite that Francis Bacon wrote 'Knowledge is Power' and printed it in his book *Meditationes Sacrae* in 1597. Finance and permission to print were the limiting factors for any communicator hundreds of years ago but the thirst for information was always strong: when Galileo's *Dialogue Concerning the Two Chief World Systems* was banned in 1633, its price increased twelve fold on the black market such was the demand for the book. Furthermore it was smuggled across the Alps to Strasbourg to be translated into Latin for distribution in Europe - preventing the spread of knowledge is like trying to stop water from flowing downhill.

Now, in the 21st century, our problem is not about getting enough information but about having too much and how to make sense of it all. The creative approach to the graphic elements of the book offered a welcome way to soothe this information overload. Weaving fact and illustration, hero and event, personal and political, the care and passion in the art direction has gone far beyond the initial vision. Possibilities opened up and excitement was palpable when we saw what could be created by integrating the printed word with creative design.

Whimsy and personal politics (from which few writers can hide) have played their part in these selections. I always kept one eye on the facts and events that most people would expect to see, but countered it with space for the individual and the curious. Ensuring a stronger female presence on the page was a challenge but what a joy to find amusing, fascinating or forgotten details about women. For example, when in the University of Rome, medical student Maria Montessori was required to perform her dissections of cadavers alone, after hours. Attending classes with men in the presence of a naked body was deemed inappropriate!

History is punctuated by conflict and resolution, yet war has made only a brief entrance to this narrative, to mark a century or decade rather than to dominate the theme. In this spirit, there can be no better time to honour than Christmas Eve in 1914, when British and German soldiers climbed out of their trenches into No Man's Land and sang carols while sharing cake and cigars. A spontaneous truce extended for hundreds of miles amongst thousands of soldiers. War and peace indeed.

Exploration, philosophy, art and science have marched inexorably forward since the dawn of civilization. A rich fabric stretches out behind us but we only need to look back for a moment to glimpse a few of its silken threads.

Bon voyage.

Alison Hackett

History is the witness that testifies to the passing of time;
it illumines reality, vitalizes memory, provides guidance in daily life
and brings us tidings of antiquity.

Cicero.

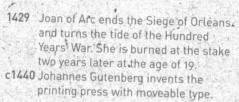

1420 Construction of the Chinese
Forbidden City is completed
in Beijing.

c1424 *Palazzo Ducale* (the Doge's
Palace) is completed in Venice.

c1425 Packs of playing cards are among
the most popular products of
Europe's first printing presses.

1429 Joan of Arc ends the Siege of Orléans,
and turns the tide of the Hundred
Years' War. She is burned at the stake
two years later at the age of 19.

c1440 Johannes Gutenberg invents the
printing press with moveable type.

c1450 The construction of
      Machu Picchu is completed.
1457 Golf is banned by King James II of
      Scotland who feels it is distracting
      young men from archery practice.
1469 Lorenzo de' Medici takes power
      in Florence.

1485 Botticelli paints *Birth of Venus*.
1492 Christopher Columbus arrives
      at an island in the Bahamas
      archipelago that he names *La Isla
      Española*, now known as Haiti and
      the Dominican Republic.

1498 Leonardo da Vinci completes
      The Last Supper.
1498 Vasco da Gama commands the
      first fleet of ships to sail from
      Europe to India.

1500 In Rome Nicolaus Copernicus observes a lunar eclipse.

c1504 Michelangelo creates the sculpture of *David*.

1503 Michel de Nostredame (Nostradamus) is born in France.

1502 Portuguese navigator João da Nova discovers the island of Saint Helena.

c1500 Johannes Trithemius writes *Steganographia* (hidden writing) a treatise on crypt

1503 Spanish forces defeat the French in the Battle of Cerignola - considered to be

c1505 Peter Henlein uses iron parts and coiled springs to start building the first

1500 Johannes Werner in Nuremberg, Germany tracks a comet taking obser

1503 Pope Alexander VI, Roderic Llançol i de Borja dies.

c1505 Leonardo da Vinci paints the *Mona Lisa*.

B.S.

649	549	333		Sat	650	626		
635	538	23		S	675	651		
646	534	S.347		P	R.700	S.676		R.
639	546	342	R.	Vir	725	701		
644	535	348		21	550	526		
646	25	343		e	575	551		
635		2 S.			S.600	R.576		S.
12	O R.			r	625	601		
647		233		M.	R.450	426		
	450	245			475	451		
634	441				R.500	S.476		R.
24		246			525	501		
		246	R.	Sol	550	326		
615				L	175	351		
642	S. 13				S.400	R.376		S.
646	447	24			425	401		
645	17	235		Ve	250			
645	446	2 S.			275			
634	442	131		S	R.300	S.		
24	439	142		A	225	226		
	20	135		M.	150	251		
Iup. S.	0	133		C	175	R. 276		R.
543	O R.	23	R.	n	S.200	301		
554	347	147		p	215	126		i.
533	342	142		D	50	151		
23	R.346	148		R	75	S.176		S.
546	549	S.143		I	R.100	201		
542	19	23		7	125	26		
539	343	150				76		R.
19	332	139			S.	101		
	346							

Grad. 16. punct Iualia 725.51

...aphy and steganography disguised as a book on magic.

...first battle won by gunpowder and small arms.

...able timepieces, later known as 'Nuremberg Eggs'.

...ons between 1st and 24th June.

c1505 Leonardo da Vinci produces the *Codex on the Flight of Birds*. **1507** Dürer completes his painting *Adam and Eve*. **1507** Explorer Amerigo Vespucci establishes that the New World is a separate land mass. A pamphlet wrongly describes him as its discoverer and America acquires its name. **1509** *De Divina Proportione* by Pacioli is published (illus

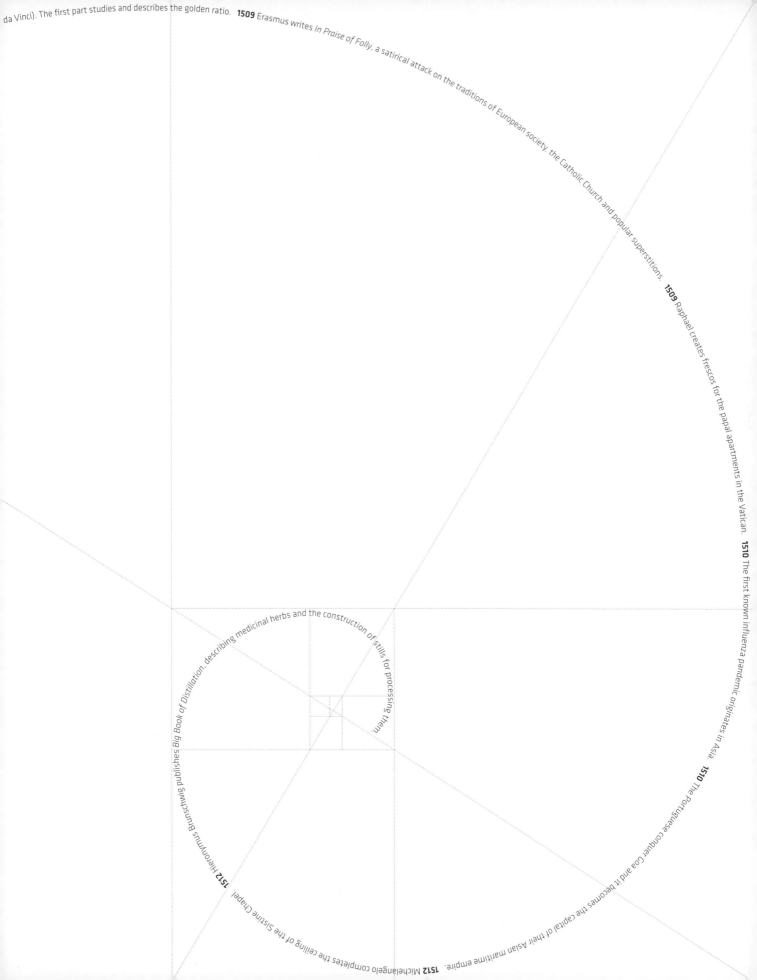

da Vinci). The first part studies and describes the golden ratio. **1509** Erasmus writes *In Praise of Folly*, a satirical attack on the traditions of European society, the Catholic Church and popular superstitions. **1509** Raphael creates frescos for the papal apartments in the Vatican. **1510** The first known influenza pandemic originates in Asia. **1510** The Portuguese conquer Goa and it becomes the capital of their Asian maritime empire. **1512** Michelangelo completes the ceiling of the Sistine Chapel. **1512** Hieronymus Brunschwig publishes *Big Book of Distillation*, describing medicinal herbs and the construction of stills for processing them.

1515 Albrec
Dürer creates
woodcut of a Rhinocer
from a written descrip
and sketch by anothe
artist, without ever seeing
the animal himself.
1516 Titian completes the
Assumption of the Virgin
his first major
commission in
Venice

1516
The
fictional
Island of
Utopia
is
described
by Thomas
Moore

1515 An
Indian
rhinoceros
arrives in Lisbon,
the first to
be seen in
Europe since
Roman
times.

1513
Johannes
Stöffler's
treatise on
the
construction
and use
of astrolabes
is published

1520 Suleyman the Magnificent becomes the tenth Sultan of the Ottoman Empire

1521 A Student rebellion takes place in the University of Erfurt, where Martin Luther had been a student and a monk from 1501-1511.

1522 The Vittoria, one of the surviving ships of Magellan's expedition, returns to spain, becoming the first ship to circumnavigate the world.

1523 Martin Luther helps Kathasina von Bora, his eventual wife, escape from the Nimbschen convent by arranging for her and 11 other nuns to be smuggled out in herring barrels.

1524 Vasco da Gama is made Governor of Portuguese India, under the title of Viceroy.

1525 In Germany the pamphlet The Twelve Articles: The Just and Fundamental Articles of All the Peasantry and Tenants of Spiritual and Temporal Powers by Whom They Think Themselves Oppressed is published, one of the first human rights related documents written in Europe.

1525 Lucas Cranach the Elder paints Cupid complaining to Venus with an inscription observing 'life's pleasure is mixed with pain'.

1525 Paracelous discovers the analgesic properties of diethyl ether.

1526 Babur becomes Mughal emperor invades northern India and captures Delhi.

1527 The Town Statues of Galway in Ireland forbid the playing of handball against the walls of the town.

1528 The Maya peoples drive the Spanish Conquistadores out of Yucatán.

c1528 The Gardens of Babur in Kabul, Afghanistan are created and later become the final resting place of the first Mughal emperor Babur.

1529 Occultist Heinrich Cornelius Agrippa publishes *Declamatio de nobilitate et praecellentia foeminei sexus* (Declamation on the Nobility and Pre-eminence of the Female Sex).

1530 The Knights of Malta are formed when Malta is given to the Knights Hospitaller by Charles V.

1530 The first book devoted to dentistry is published in Germany: Artzney büchlein: wider allerlei kranckeyten und gebrechen der tzeen *(The little medicinal book for all kinds of diseases and infirmities of the teeth)*.

1531 One of the earliest lighthouses in the world, the Kõpu Lighthouse on the Estonian island of Hiiumaa, is first lit. It remains in continuous use into the 21st century.

1532 Francisco Pizarro defeats and captures Inca emperor Atahualpa.

1532 Henry VIII builds a court for the game of Royal Tennis, now known as Real Tennis, at Hampton Court Palace.

1533 Hans Holbein the Younger paints *The Ambassadors*.

1534 Explorer Jacques Cartier claims the area now known as Quebec, for France, describing it as Kanata, the Huron-Iroquois word for village.

1535 Jacopo Berengario da Carpi publishes *Anatomia Carpi*, the first anatomical text with illustrations, in Bologna.

1535 Lima is founded as la Ciudad de los Reyes, City of Kings.

1535 Leonhart Fuchs grows medicinal plants in the botanical garden of the University of Tübingen.

1535 Fray Tomás de Berlanga discovers the Galapagos Islands when his boat is blown off course en route to Peru.

1536 Henry VIII is injured in a jousting accident from which he never fully recovers.

1536 Adam Ries publishes a book of tables for calculating everyday prices with a foreword noting his concern 'that the poor common man not be cheated when buying bread'.

1537 Niccolò Tartaglia publishes La Nova Scientia applying mathematics to the study of ballistics.

1537 The reign of Cosimo I de' Medici begins.

1538 Maddalena Casulana composes First Book of Madrigals for Four Voices – the first female composer to have her music printed and published in the West.

1538 Titian paints Venus of Urbino.

1538 Hans Holbein the Younger paints portraits of potential Queens for Henry VIII including Christina of Denmark and Anne of Cleves.

1539 Johannes Baptista Montanus, Professor of medicine at the University of Padua, introduces bedside examination into the curriculum, integrating theory and practice.

1540 Andreas Vesalius shows in dissections in public that female and male skeletons have the same number of ribs.

1540 Ethiopian music notation is developed.

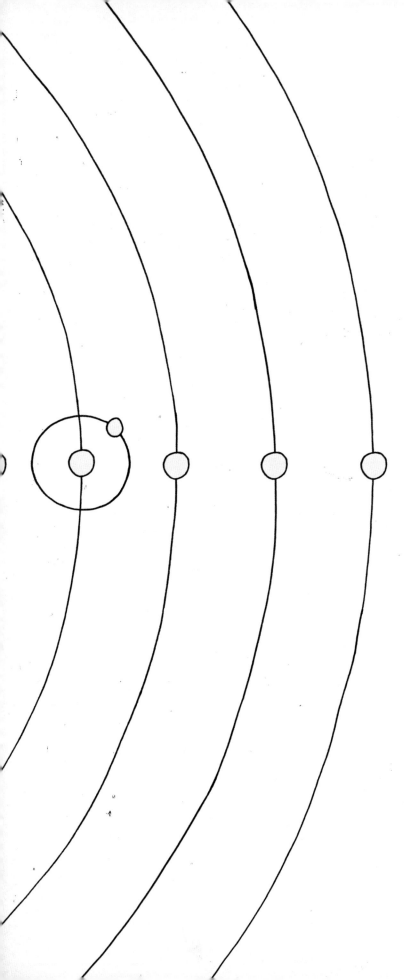

1540 Waltham Abbey is the final priory to fall in the dissolution of the monasteries.

1540 The Society of Jesus (Jesuits) is approved by Pope Paul III, in his bull *Regimini militantis Ecclesiae*.

1541 Ottoman Sultan Suleiman the Magnificent seals off The Golden Gate in Jerusalem.

1541 Gerardus Mercator makes his first globe.

1541 Elia Levita's chivalric romance, the *Bovo-Bukh*, is the earliest published secular work in Yiddish.

1543 Japan's first contact with the West occurs when a Portuguese ship, blown off its course to China, lands in Japan.

1543 Nicolaus Copernicus proposes that the earth is not the centre of the Universe in *De Revolutionibus Orbium Celestium*.

1543 *On the Fabric of the Human Body in Seven books* by Andreas Vesalius is published.

1545 The world's first Botanical Garden, still in its original location, is established in Padua.

c1545 Silver is discovered at Potosí, Bolivia.

1545 The Council of Trent opens.

c1545 Il Bronzino paints *Venus, Cupid, Folly and Time.*

c1545 In China, failure of the harvest in the Henan province causes famine.

1546 *The sea monk* is the name given to a sea animal found off the eastern coast of the Danish island of Zealand. Many now believe this to have been the giant squid *Architeuthis.*

1546 A Persian miniature made during the Safavid dynasty shows Persian courtiers on horseback playing a game of polo.

1546 Girolamo Fracastoro proposes that epidemic diseases are caused by transferable tiny particles or 'spores' that can transmit infection by direct or indirect contact.

1547 Ivan IV (Ivan the Terrible) is the first person to be crowned as Tsar of All the Russias.

1547 In Malaysia, Francis Xavier, one of the first seven Jesuits and student of Ignatius of Loyola, meets a Japanese man named Anjirō who becomes the first Japanese Christian.

1548 The Ming Dynasty government of China issues a decree banning all foreign trade and closes down all seaports along the coast.

1548 Firearms are used for the first time on the battlefield in Japan.

1549 The spire of Lincoln Cathedral in England is blown down, leaving St. Olaf's Church, Tallinn, in Estonia as the world's tallest structure (125m) until 1625.

1550 The laying out of the gardens at the Villa d'Este in Tivoli begins.

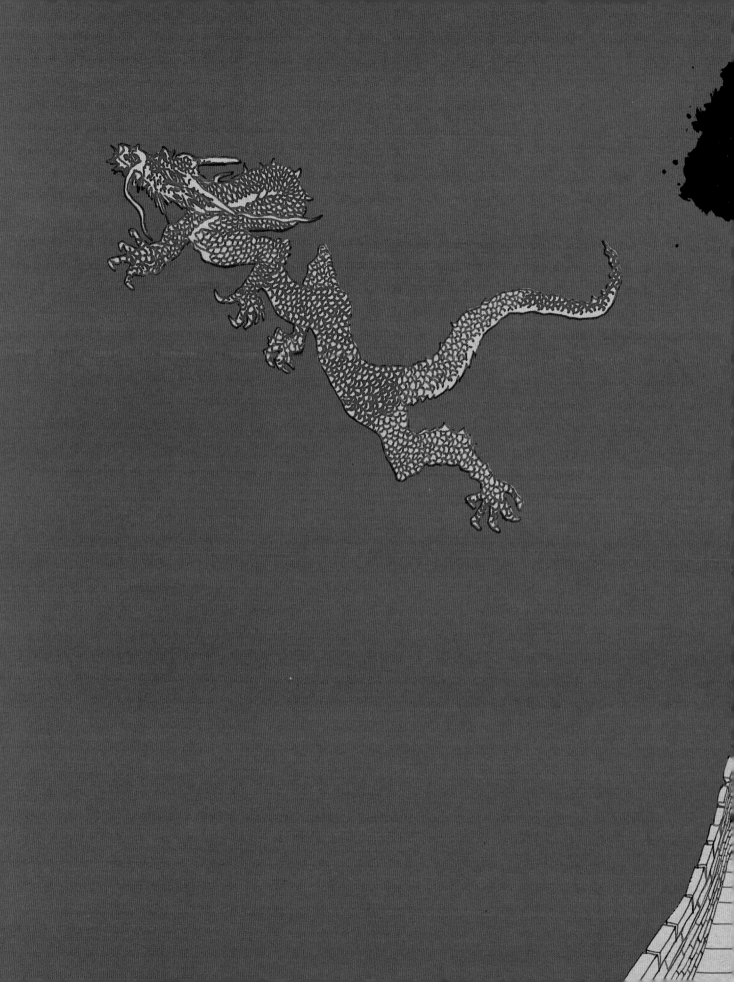

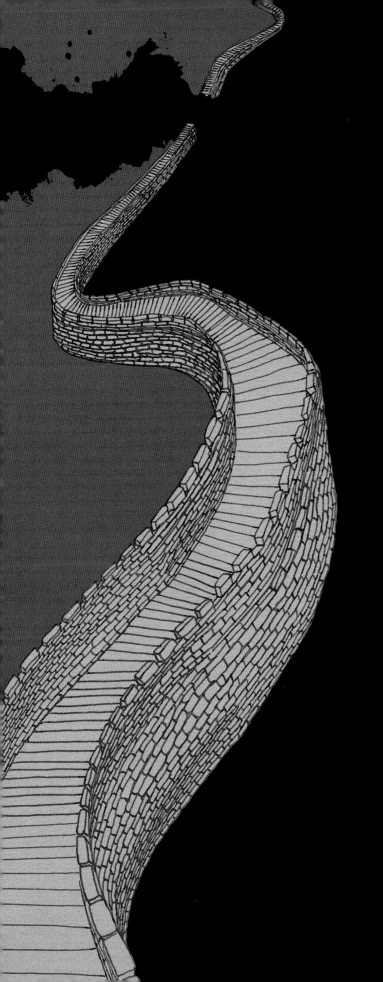

1550 Andrea Palladio designs the *Rotunda* in Vincenza.

1550 Altan Khan, a descendant of Kublai Khan, breaches the Great Wall of China and besieges Beijing.

1551 The first recorded Commedia dell'Arte performances take place in Rome.

1551 Pieter Aertsen paints *Butcher's Stall.*

1551 *Historiae Animalium* (Histories of the Animals) by Conrad Gesner is published - an encyclopedic work describing all the animals known.

1553 The first book on the benefits of physical exercise for health, *Libro del Exercicio*, is published in Spain.

1553 *Company of Merchant Adventurers to New Lands* is the first joint-stock company to be chartered in London.

1553 Lady Jane Grey is proclaimed Queen of England, a position she holds for nine days.

1555 The first edition of *Les Propheties* by Nostradamus is published.

1555 French forces occupy the harbour at the mouth of the Janeiro river in Brazil. Two years later, Portugal will regain control and establish the city of Rio de Janeiro.

c 1555 The illuminated tugra of Sultan Suleyman is created.

1556 Guillaume Rondelet's anatomical drawing of a sea urchin is the earliest extant depiction of an invertebrate.

1556 Akbar the Great becomes the third Mughal Emperor at the age of 13.

1556 The first printing press in India is introduced at Saint Paul's College in Goa.

1556 Phillip II becomes King of Spain. During his reign Spanish colonies, including the Philippine Islands, are claimed in all the known continents.

1557 Spain becomes bankrupt, throwing German banking houses into chaos.

1557 German adventurer Hans Staden publishes an account of his detention by the Tupí people of Brazil - *True Story and Description of a Country of Wild, Naked, Grim, Man-eating People in the New World, America.*

1557 At the Battle of St. Quentin French surgeon Ambroise Paré notes that maggots assist in the healing of wounds.

1558 *Magia Naturalis* (Natural Magic), a work of popular science by Giambattista della Porta, is published in Naples.

1559 Lorenzo Valla's book of 1440 which exposed the fact that the Donation of Constantine was a forgery, is placed on the Index *Librorum Prohibitorum.*

1559 Jean Nicot describes the medicinal properties of tobacco and introduces it in the form of snuff to the French court.

c1559 John Shakespeare (father of the playwright) whitewashes over the religious frescoes in the Guild Chapel of the Holy Cross in Stratford-upon-Avon following the royal injunction calling for all 'superstition and idolatry' be removed from places of worship.

1560 The oldest surviving violin (dated inside), known as the *Charles IX*, is made in Cremona, in northern Italy.

1560 - 1565

1560 Building of the Uffizi palace in Florence commences. It is designed by Giorgio Vasari for Cosimo I de' Medici as the offices for the Florentine magistrates.

1561 Ruy López de Segura describes new techniques for playing chess in his publication Book of the Liberal Invention and Art of the Game Chess.

1562 Fray Diego de Landa, the acting Bishop of Yucatán, burns the sacred books of the Maya.

1562 Giacomo Barozzi da Vignola publishes Rules of the Five Orders of Architecture.

c1563 Tower of Babel is painted by Pieter Breugel the Elder.

1563 Garcia de Orta publishes Colóquios dos Simples e Drogas da India in Goa, the first text in a Western language on tropical medicine and drugs, including a classic description of cholera.

1564 Ivan Fyodorov and Pyotr Mstislavets establish the Moscow Print Yard and start to publish works using moveable type. Persecuted for this by the traditional Muscovite scribes they are forced to flee to the Grand Duchy of Lithuania after their printing workshop is burned down.

1564 Michelangelo dies. Galileo is born. Shakespeare is born.

1564 An early form of the pencil is invented when a huge graphite mine is discovered in Borrowdale, Cumbria, England.

1564 Authors and printers are excommunicated if they print any works from the list of prohibited books.

c1564 Naples prohibits kissing in public under penalty of death.

1565 The College of Physicians of London is empowered to carry out human dissections.

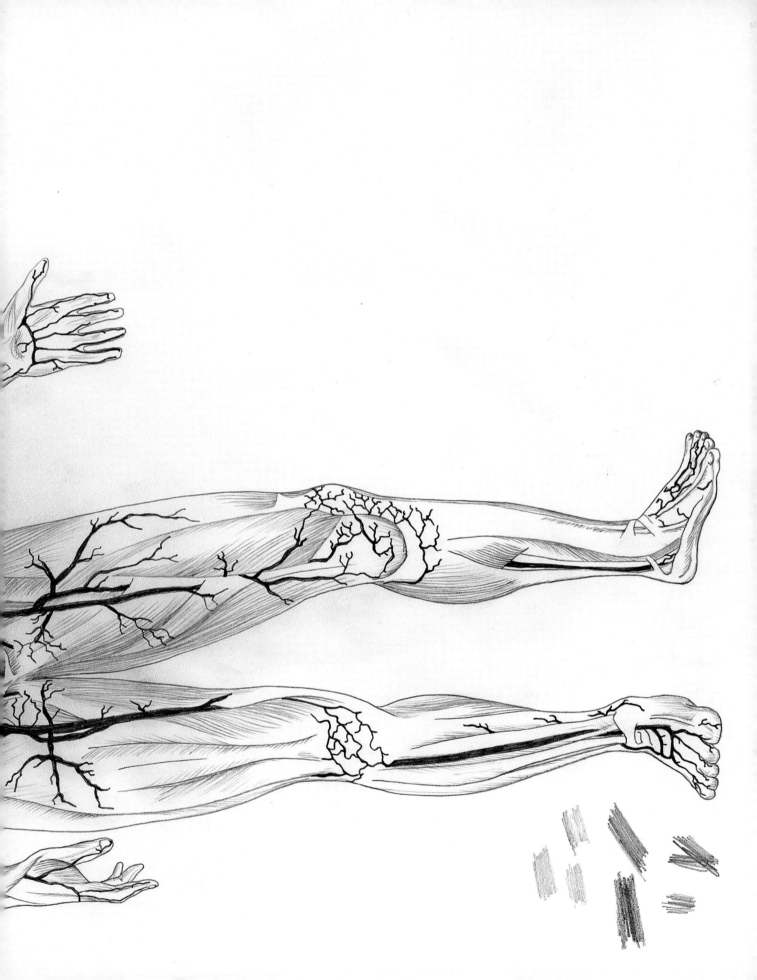

1566 Calvinists destroys many religious works of art in Belgium, the Netherlands, and Luxembourg.

1569 The Mercator projection, a cylindrical map projection created by the Flemish geographer and cartographer Gerardus Mercator, is published.

1570s Giuseppe Arcimboldo paints The Librarian.

1569 The first recorded lottery in England is performed at the west door of St. Pauls Cathedral. Each share costs ten shillings and the proceeds are used for public works such as repairing harbours.

1566 Danish astronomer Tycho Brahe loses part of his nose in a sword duel due to a quarrel over the legitimacy of a mathematical formula.

1567 1200 watchtower are constructed on the Great Wall of China in order to warn of approaching Mongol r

1565 The first Martello tower, the Torra di Mortella is completed as part of the Genovese defence system i

1566 The Spanish doubloon is first minted during the reign of Phillip II of Spain.

1569 The Bible is printed in Castilian for the first time.

1566 The Ottomans build the first bridge to cross the Neretva river (Bosnia - Herzegovina). The reconstructed bridge is now known as Stari Most (Old Brid

1566 Pope Pius V orders the expulsion of Prostitutes from Rome.

Corsica.

Mostar

1570 John Shakespeare (father of William) seeks the title of gentleman and applies for his coat-of-arms. 1573 The first Spanish galleon laden with silver and applies for in exchange for porcelain and silk in China, lands at Manila to trade in the Philippines. 1570 Theatrum Orbis Terrarum (Theatre of the world) by Abraham Ortelius is printed - an early modern of the atlas. 1570 Andrea Palladio's treatise, Four Books of Architecture, is published.

1574 La Alameda in Seville, Spain is laid out as Europe's first public garden. 1572 Cornelius Gemma is the first European to observe and record an illustration of a Supernova (in the constellation Cassiopeia). 1572 Vilcabamba in Peru, the last independent remnant of the Inca Empire, is conquered by Spain.

1572 Raphael Bombelli calculates using imaginary numbers. 1573 The Muromachi period ends when the 15th and last shogun of this line, Ashikago Yoshiaki, is driven out of the capital in Kyoto by Oda Nobunaga.

1575 Nicholas Hilliard paints a portrait of Elizabeth I the Pelican Portrait. The pelican represented on her brooch, feeding her offspring with her own blood, is a symbol of the self-sacrifice of Elizabeth as mother of the nation.

c1575 Jacopo Tintoretto paints *The Origin of the Milky Way.*
1575 Ambroise Paré, the father of modern surgery, writes 'There are five duties of surgery: to remove what is superfluous, to restore what has been dislocated, to separate what has grown together, to reunite what has been divided, and to redress the defects of nature.'

1576 James Burbage builds *The Theatre,* the first permanent public playhouse in London.
1577 Building begins on Tycho Brahe's observatory called Uraniborg (heavenly castle) on the island of Hven in the Danish Sound.
1578 Sonam Gyrso becomes the first officially recognized Dalai Lama of Tibet.

3. Restore

5. Redress

1579   Giambologna begins his sculpture,
the *Rape of the Sabine Women*.

1579   Francis Drake lands in North California and gives the
name Nova Albion (New England) to the region of the
Pacific coast that he claims for England.

1580   The Ostrog Bible, the first complete Bible
printed in a Slavic language, is published.

1580   The Istanbul observatory Taqi al-Din is
destroyed by Sultan Selim II.

1580   A broadside ballad is registered at the London
Stationers' Company with the title *A Newe Northen
Dittye of ye Ladye Greene Sleves*.

2. Seperate

1. Remove

4. Reunite

1580 The *concerto delle donne*, a group of professional female singers, is founded by Alfonso II, Duke of Ferrara.

1580 The first session of the Jewish *Vaad* (Council of Four Lands) is held in Lublin, Poland.

1581 The Ming Dynasty Chancellor of China imposes the *Single Whip Reform*, in which taxes (to be paid in silver) are assessed on properties recorded in the land census.

1582 John Dee becomes a recognised expert in mathematics, astronomy and navigation while also practicing the art of scrying - looking into a translucent ball or crystal to see spiritual visions.

1582 Italy, Poland-Lithuania, Portugal, and Spain become the first countries to change from the Julian to the Gregorian calendar, skipping 11 days (Thursday 4th October is followed by Friday 15th Oct.)

1583 Carolus Clusius publishes the first book on Alpine flora.

c1583 Lavinia Fontana paints *Newborn Baby in a Crib*. Despite bearing eleven children she continues to paint to support the family while her husband serves as her assistant.

1584 The Jesuit China missionary, Matteo Ricci produces the first European-style map of the world in Chinese now known as 'the impossible black tulip of cartography' as no prints of the map survive.

1585 Palladio's *Teatro Olimpico* in Vicenza is completed with trompe-l'œil onstage scenery to give the appearance of long streets receding to a distant horizon. It is the oldest surviving stage set still in existence.

c1585 A portrait is painted of Christopher Marlowe with the motto inscribed: QVOD ME NVTRIT ME DESTRVIT (that which nourishes me destroys me).

1585 Chocolate
is introduced to
Europe commercially.

1585 Shakespeare's
twins, Hamnet
and Judith, are
born.

1590 Giuseppe Arcimboldo
creates a portrait of Rudolf II as Vertumnus
(Roman God of the seasons)
using fruit, vegetables and flowers in the painting.

1586 Mary Queen of Scots, the Catholic cousin
of the Protestant Queen Elizabeth I, is tried for treason.

1586 Simon Stevin, a Flemish mathematician,
demonstrates that two objects of different weight
fall with the same speed.

1587 Construction begins on the Pont Neuf,
the oldest standing bridge across the Seine in Paris.

1589 Shakespeare writes his first play, Comedy of Errors.

1587 The Banco della Piazza di Rialto is opened
in Venice to hold merchants' funds on safe deposit
and enable financial transactions to be
made without the physical transfer of coins.

1588 In Japan Hideyoshi forbids ordinary
peasants from owning weapons and starts
a sword hunt to confiscate arms. The
swords are melted down to create
a statue of the Buddha.

1588 With the Spanish Armada in sight
Queen Elizabeth I rallies her troops
with the words 'I know I have the body but of
a weak and feeble woman; but I have
the heart and stomach of a king.'

1590 In the Netherlands, glass lenses are adapted for use in the first microscopes and telescopes.

1594 The first tulip bulbs planted in Holland come into flower.

1591 François Viète introduces the new algebra using letters as parameters in equations.

1594 St. Paul's College in Macau is founded by Je

1594 The Cardsharps is painted by Caravaggio.

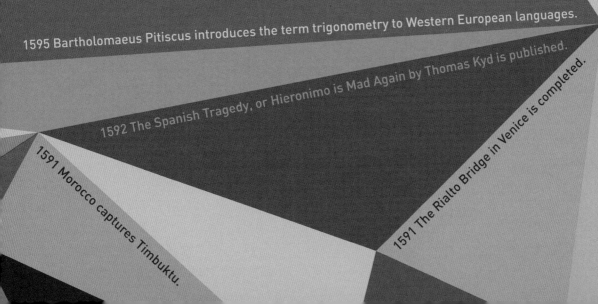

...e first western style university in the Far East.

1592 Trinity College Dublin is founded.

1590 The first half of The Fairie Queen by Edmund Spenser is published.

1594 The first permanent anatomical theatre is opened at the University of Padua.

1595 Bartholomaeus Pitiscus introduces the term trigonometry to Western European languages.

1592 The Spanish Tragedy, or Hieronimo is Mad Again by Thomas Kyd is published.

1591 The Rialto Bridge in Venice is completed.

1591 Morocco captures Timbuktu.

1595 In the first Italian book on obstetrics Scipione Mercurio advocates caesarean operation in cases of contracted pelvis.

1597 Francis Bacon writes 'Knowledge is power' in *Meditationes Sacrae* (Sacred Meditations).

1597 In Japan, Hideyoshi has twenty-six Christians executed by public crucifixion.

1597 Galileo invents the Geometric and Military Compass – the device functions as an early mathematical calculator.

1598 *Dafne* by Jacopo Peri, the earliest known work that could be considered a modern opera, is performed during *Carnevale* in Florence.

1598 The word 'coffee' enters the English language via the Dutch word 'koffie'.

ILEDGE

1598 In a manuscript, the Guildford
Book of Court uses the word
'creckett' for a game played in
Guildford school.

1599 'The evil that men do lives
after them/the good is oft
interred with their bones',
Mark Anthony eulogises Julius
Caesar in Shakespeare's play.

1599 The Globe Theatre is built in
London. A flag raised over the
theatre indicates the type of
play being performed on any
day – white for comedy, black
for tragedy and red for history.

1600 The navigator William Adams
is the first Englishman to reach
Japan. He becomes a key
advisor to *shogun* Tokugawa
Ieyasu and builds Japan's first
western-style ships.

1600 Laying out begins on the parterre in Castello Ruspoli, Italy.

1600 Dominican friar and astronomer Giordano Bruno is burned at the stake for proposing, amongst other things, that the Sun is a star.

c1600 Sumo wrestling becomes a spectator sport in Japan.

1601 The Jesuit, Matteo Ricci becomes the first European to enter the Forbidden City in Beijing, China.

1601 The Battle of Kinsale in Ireland.

1602 Felix Plater publishes *Praxis Medica* presenting a method for classifying diseases by their symptoms.

1602 The Confucian scholar Li Zhi is imprisoned in China for spreading the 'dangerous idea' that women are the intellectual equals of men and should be given equal opportunity in education.

1602 Caravaggio paints *The Taking of Christ*.

1602 The Dutch East India Company is formed as a joint-stock company with shares that are readily tradable.

c1604 Marie Venier is the first female actress to appear on stage in Paris.

1604 The Sikh Holy Scripture *Guru Granth Sahib* is compiled by Guru Arjan.

1604 *Doctor Faustus* by Christopher Marlowe is published. It is based on the story of *Faust*, a man who sells his soul to the devil for power and knowledge.

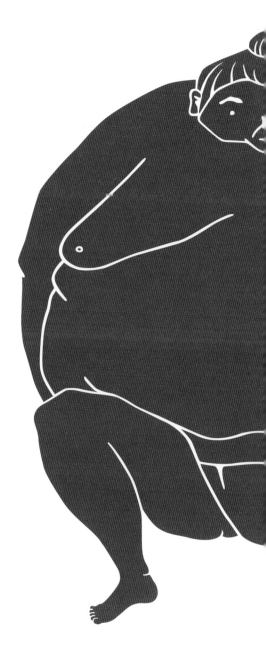

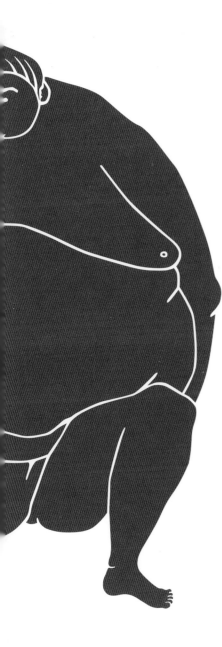

1607 The Bank of Genoa fails after the announcement of national bankruptcy in Spain.
1605 Don Quixote part I by Miguel de Cervantes is published.

1605 THE PLOT TO BLOW UP THE ENGLISH HOUSES OF PARLIAMENT IS FOILED WHEN GUY FAWKES IS DISCOVERED GUARDING 36 BARRELS OF GUNPOWDER IN A CELLAR BELOW THE PARLIAMENT BUILDING.

1607 CLAUDIO MONTEVERDI WRITES L'ORFEO, ONE OF THE FIRST GREAT OPERAS.

1605 THE WORLD'S FIRST NEWSPAPER, RELATION ALLER FÜRNEMMEN UND GEDENCKWÜRDIGEN HISTORIEN (COLLECTION OF ALL DISTINGUISHED AND COMMEMORABLE NEWS) IS PUBLISHED IN STRASBOURG.

1607 FLIGHT OF THE EARLS: HUGH O'NEILL AND RORY O'DONNELL FLEE IRELAND HEADING FOR SPAIN.

C1610 PETER PAUL RUBENS PAINTS THE MASSACRE OF THE INNOCENTS. THE WORK WILL BE SOLD AT AUCTION AT SOTHEBY'S, LONDON IN 2002 FOR £49.5 MILLION.

1609 JOHANNES KEPLER PUBLISHES HIS FIRST TWO LAWS OF PLANETARY MOTION IN ASTRONOMIA NOVA.

1610 GALILEO CONSTRUCTS A REFRACTING TELESCOPE AND OBSERVES THE MOONS OF JUPITER, NAMING THEM IO, EUROPA, GANYMEDE AND CALLISTO.

1607 HAMLET IS PERFORMED ABOARD THE EAST INDIA COMPANY SHIP RED DRAGON WHILE ANCHORED OFF THE COAST OF SIERRA LEONE.

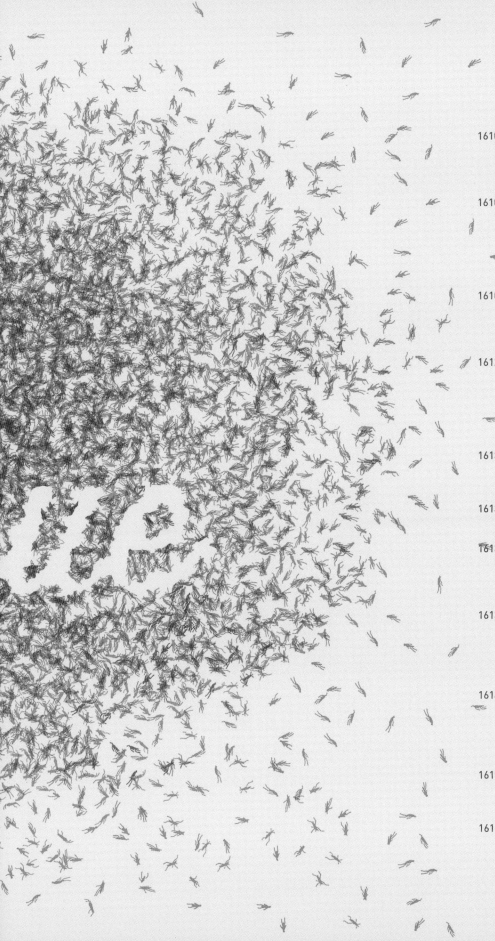

1610 Galileo shows the Doge of Venice how to use his refracting telescope to see ships approaching from far out at sea.

1610 Edward Coke, Chief Justice of England's Court of Common Pleas, affirms the supremacy of the common law, which limits the power of parliament as well as the king.

1610 The Portuguese colony of Brazil accumulates wealth through the production and export of up to 71,000 tons of sugar a year.

1612 Artemisia Gentileschi paints *Judith Slaying Holofernes*, a classic scene from the Bible. Gentileschi draws herself as Judith and her mentor Agostino Tassi (who was tried in court for her rape) as Holofernes.

1613 Mikhail Romanov becomes Tsar of Russia, establishing the Romanov dynasty.

1613 A locust swarm destroys La Camarque, France.

1613 Japanese shogun Tokugawa Ieyasu decrees that William Adams the pilot is dead and that samurai Miura Anjin is born.

1613 Pocahontas is captured by the English. She converts to Christianity and marries John Rolfe, a tobacco planter, in Jamestown Virginia the following year.

1614 In the last years of his life El Greco completes *The Opening of the Fifth Seal*, believed to be the prime source of inspiration for Picasso's *Les Demoiselles d'Avignon* (1907).

1615 A London armsmaster begins offering public lessons in fisticuffs to the gentry.

1616 The Sultan Ahmed Mosque in Istanbul (the Blue Mosque) is completed.

1616   Moralist writer John Deacon publishes a quarto entitled *Tobacco Tortured or the Filthie Fume of Tobacco Refined.*

6⁻0

1616   Dutch traders smuggle the coffee plant out of Mocha, a port in Yemen on the Red Sea, and cultivate it at the Amsterdam Botanical Gardens.

c1616   Astronomer Johannes Kepler is charged with witchcraft. His mother is charged with the same offence several years later.

1616   The first non-aristocratic, free public school in Europe is opened in Frascati, Italy.

5⁻0

4⁻0

1616
NAME: KEPLER J
HT 5˝10   WT 142
WITCHCRAFT

1616 *De Revolutionibus* by Copernicus is suspended until corrections are made. Galileo makes the corrections to his copy very lightly.

6⁻0

1616 The first performance of the play *Christmas, His Masque* by Ben Jonson takes place. Father Christmas is dressed as a jolly figure in a

comical costume suggesting that he is descended from the presenter of the medieval mid-winter festival called the 'Feast of Fools'.

1618 Ivan Petlin, a Siberian Cossack, is the first Russian to travel to China on an official mission.

1618 The Defenestration of Prague triggers the Thirty Years War.

5⁻0

1620 The Pilgrim Fathers arrive at Plymouth Rock on the *Mayflower*.

1620 A merry-go-round is seen at a fair in Philippapolis, Turkey – one of the earliest records of a carousel at a fair.

4⁻0

1620

NAME: KEPLER K

HT 5˙6   WT 122

WITCHCRAFT

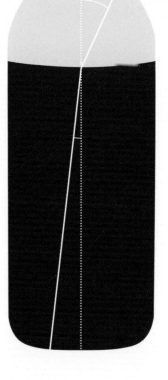

1620 Cornelis Drebbel builds the first navigable submarine while working for the English Royal Navy.

1620 The oldest stone church in French North America, *Notre-Dame-des-Anges*, is founded in Quebec, Canada.

1621 Willebrord Snellius van Royen describes the law of refraction later known as Snell's Law.

1622 *Congregatio de Propaganda Fide* is set up to spread the Roman Catholic faith and counter the expansion of Protestant colonization.

1623 The first American temperance law is enacted in Virginia.

1623 *Mr. William Shakespeares Comedies, Histories, & Tragedies* – the First Folio is published.

1623 *Secret History* by Procopius, written in the 6th Century, is discovered in the Vatican Library.

1623 A psychiatric treatise *Maladie d'Amour ou Mélancolie Érotique* by Jacques Ferrand is published.

1624 Portuguese Jesuit priest António de Andrade becomes the first European to enter Tibet.

1624 Ana de Sousa Nzingha Mbande becomes Queen Nzinga of Ndongo and Matamba (now Angola).

1624 Frans Hals paints the portrait now known as the *Laughing Cavalier*.

1625 Francis Bacon writes 'he that will not apply new remedies must expect new evils' in his publication *The Essayes or Counsels, Civill and Morall*.

1626 Peter Minuit buys Manhattan from Native Americans (thought to be the Lenape tribe) for trade goods valued at 60 guilders.

1627 The last recorded auroch, the ancestor of domestic cattle, dies in the Jaktorow Forest in Poland

1628 The War of the Mantuan Succession begins, caused by the extinction of the direct male line of the House of Gonzaga

1628 William Harvey describes the circulation of *bl*

1625 Galileo writes about the nature of indivisible points.

...ority dispute about the invention with Richard Delamain

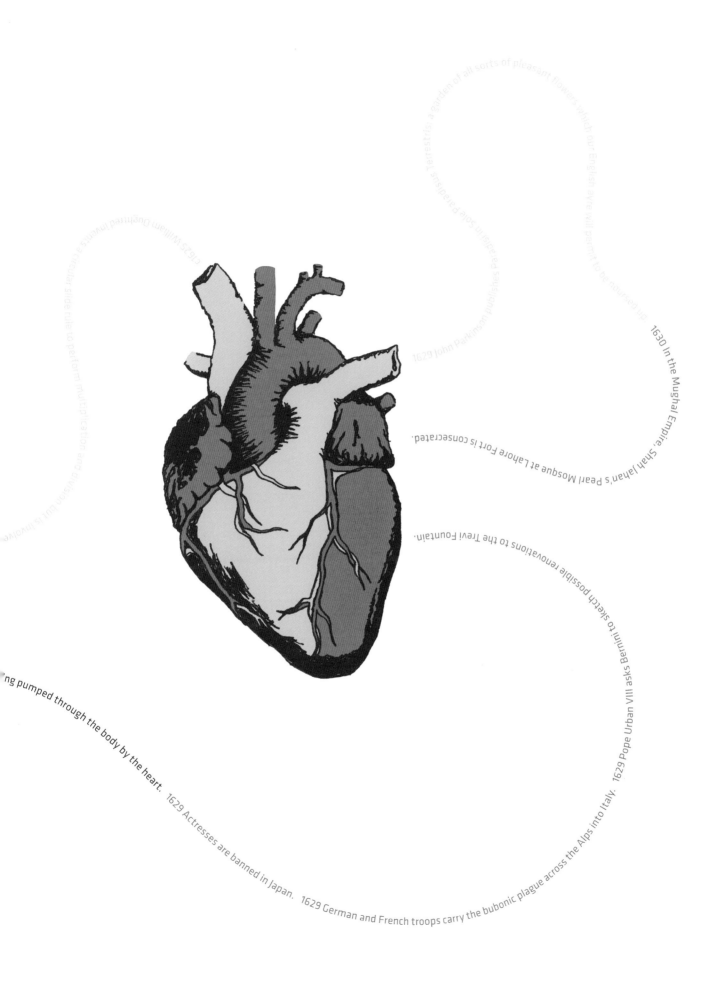

c1625 William Oughtred invents a circular slide rule to perform multiplication and division but is involve[...]

c1625 William Oughtred invents a garden of all sorts of pleasant flowers which our English ayre will permit to be noursed up

1629 John Parkinson publishes Paradisi in Sole Paradisus Terrestris; a garden of all sorts of pleasant flowers which our English ayre will permit to be noursed up

1630 In the Mughal Empire, Shah Jahan's Pearl Mosque at Lahore Fort is consecrated.

1629 Pope Urban VIII asks Bernini to sketch possible renovations to the Trevi Fountain.

...ng pumped through the body by the heart.   1629 Actresses are banned in Japan.   1629 German and French troops carry the bubonic plague across the Alps into Italy.

1630 Pierre de Fermat studies the curve later known as the Witch of Agnesi.

1630 Cornelius Drebbel produces an early form of magic lantern or slide projector.

1630 Massachusetts Bay Colony outlaws the possession of cards, dice, and gaming tables.

1631 William Oughtred introduces the multiplication sign (×) and the proportion sign (::)

1631 La Gazette, the first French newspaper, is founded.

1631 Algerian pirates sack Baltimore in County Cork, Ireland.

1632 Construction of the Taj Mahal begins.

1632 Rembrandt paints *The Anatomy Lesson of Dr. Nicolaes Tulp*.

1633 The first Protestant cathedral to be built in Europe, St Columb's Cathedral in Derry, Ireland is completed.

1633 Galileo's banned publication *The Dialogue* increases in price from ½ scudo to 6 scudo on the black market. It is smuggled across the Alps to Strasbourg to be translated into Latin for distribution in Europe.

1634 *The Story of Stories* by Giambattista Basile is published posthumously. It includes the tale of Cenerentola and the character Zezolla – an early version of *Cinderella*.

1635 Chen Hongshou creates an ink and colour self-portrait.

1635 In Japan, all foreign commerce is confined to the artificial island of Dejima in Nagasaki Bay.

1636 New College (Harvard University) is established as the first college to be founded in North America.

1636 John Milton and Thomas Hobbes are amongst the many supporters to visit Galileo while he is under house arrest in Italy.

1636 King Christian of Denmark gives an order that all beggars that are able to work must be sent to Brinholmen, to build ships or to work as galley rowers.

1637 Pierre de Fermat makes a note in a document margin about a proof that will later be known as *Fermat's Last Theorem*.

1637 The first recorded European-made eyeglasses to enter China (38,421 pairs) arrive on six ships.

1637 René Descartes writes the phrase; *cogito ergo sum* (I am thinking, therefore I exist).

1637 Tulip Mania reaches its peak – some single tulip bulbs sell for more than 10 times the annual income of a skilled craftsman.

1638 Pedro Teixeira makes the first ascent of the Amazon River, from its mouth to Quito, Ecuador.

1638 The Beijing Gazette makes an official switch in its production process of newspapers, from woodblock printing to movable type printing.

1640 Rembrandt paints *Self Portrait at age 34*, believed to be inspired by Titian's similarly posed painting c1509 *A man with a quilted sleeve*.

BASEL PROBL

$$\sum_{n=1}^{\infty}$$

$$\lim_{n \to +\infty} \frac{\frac{1}{n^2}}{M}$$

1645 *Theater of the World, or a New Atlas of Maps and Representations of All Regions*, edited by Willem and Joan Blaeu is printed.

1645 Wallpaper begins to replace tapestries as a wall decoration.

1646 Massachusetts enacts the death penalty for having a rebellious child.

1647 England's Puritan rulers ban Christmas. The following year they order that all playhouses and theatres are to be pulled down, all players seized and whipped, and anyone caught attending a play fined five shillings.

1648 The Russian explorer Semyon Dezhnyov reaches the area later named as the Bering Strait.

1648 Jan Baptista van Helmont introduces the word 'gas' (from the Greek word khaos) into the vocabulary.

1650 The first modern Palio horserace is held in Siena.

1650 Ann Greene, who had been hanged for infanticide in Edinburgh, wakes up on the autopsy table and is pardoned.

c1650 Diego Velázquez creates the *Portrait of Pope Innocent X.*

1650 The word 'obesity' is used for the first time in *Via Recta ad Vitam Longam* (Straight Road to Long Life) by Tobias Venner.

1650 *The Tenth Muse Lately Sprung Up in America* by Anne Bradstreet is the first volume of poetry to be published in the British North American colonies.

1650 Three-wheeled wheelchairs are invented in Nuremberg by watchmaker Stephen Farfler.

1651 Laws are passed in Massachusetts forbidding poor people from adopting excessive styles of dress.

1651 Thomas Hobbes book *Leviathan* establishes the foundation for most western political philosophy from the perspective of social contract theory.

c1651 Diego Velázquez paints the *Rokeby Venus* - the only surviving nude by this artist.

1652 George Fox forms The Religious Society of Friends (Quakers) with the philosophy: 'God does not dwell in temples or institutions made with hands, but freely in the hearts of men.'

1652 The Dutch establish the first European settlement in South Africa at Cape Town.

1652 The minuet comes into fashion at French court.

1654 Otto von Guericke demonstrates the force of atmospheric pressure using Magdeburg hemispheres before Ferdinand III, Holy Roman Emperor, and the Imperial Diet in Regensburg.

1654 Blaise Pascal lays the foundations of Probability Theory.

1654 Ferdinando II de' Medici sponsors the first weather-observing network with meteorological stations in Florence, Cutigliano, Vallombrosa, Bologna, Parma, Milan, Innsbruck, Osnabrück, Paris and Warsaw.

1655 The *Bibliotheca Thysiana* is erected, the only surviving 17th century example in the Netherlands of a building designed as a library.

1655 John Wallis introduces the symbol ∞ to represent infinity. 1656 The Black Madonna icon (Our Lady of Częstochowa) is crowned as Queen and Protector of Poland after a small force of monks from the Jasna Gora monastery fight off Swedish invaders and save their sacred icon. 1656 Diego Velázquez paints Las Meninas on which Picasso bases a series of 58 paintings over 300 years later. 1656 The Hospice de la Salpêtrière hospital in Paris is commissioned to replace a structure that had previously been used as a gunpowder factory, a prison and a holding place for the poor. 1656 Christiaan Huygens designs the first working pendulum clock. 1657 Stockholm's Banco, the precursor to the central bank of Sweden, is founded and will become the first European bank to print banknotes four years later. 1657 The first eleven Quaker settlers arrive in New Amsterdam (later New York) and are allowed to practice their faith. 1657 Thomas Middleton's tragedy Women Beware Women is published posthumously. 1659 Parisian police raid a monastery and send the monks to prison for eating meat and drinking wine during Lent. 1659 Louis XIV meets his future wife, the Spanish Infanta, Maria Theresa at Isla de los Faisanes, a river island in the Basque country. 1660 The Alawite dynasty takes over in Morocco. 1660 Samuel Pepys has his first cup of tea, an event recorded in his diary.

1660 The great west window of Winchester Cathedral is reconstructed in a mosaic style using glass fragments dating from 1330 – an early prefiguring of collage art.

1660 The first female actor appears on the stage as Desdemona in *Othello*, following the re-opening of the theatres in England.

1662 Mr Punch of *Punch and Judy* makes his first recorded appearance.

1662 A short-lived experiment with the first public buses holding 8 passengers begins in Paris.

1662 Boyle's Law describes the inverse relationship between volume and pressure of a gas at a constant temperature.

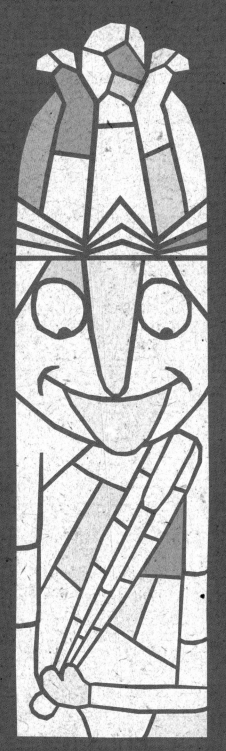

1664 Kronenbourg lager is first produced.

1664 The palace and gardens at Versailles are commissioned by Louis XIV.

1665 Robert Hooke discovers that cork is made of 'tiny little rooms' which he calls 'cells'.

1665 Margaret Porteous is the first person on record to die in the Great Plague of London.

1665 Jan Vermeer paints *Girl with a Pearl Earring.*

1665 Domenico Cassini, astronomy professor at Bologna University, refines the telescope and traces the meridian line in Patronio.

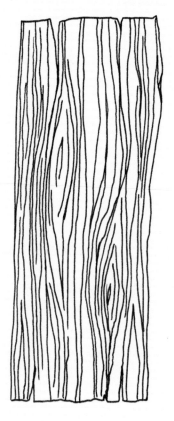
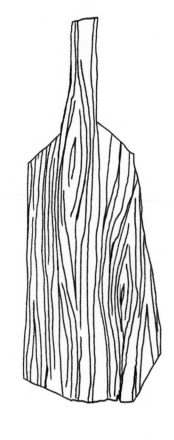
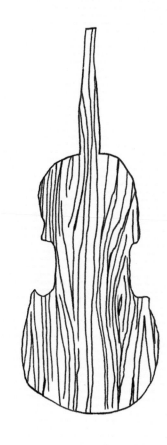

1665 *The Royal Game of Chesse Play* by Gioacchino Greco, the first professional chess player, is published posthumously.

1665 Gabriël Metsu completes his painting *Lady Reading a Letter* the same year that Jan Vermeer paints *A Lady Writing a Letter*.

1666 Molière's comedy, *The Misanthrope*, premières at the Théâtre du Palais-Royal in Paris.

1666 Isaac Newton develops his Method of Fluxions (a version of calculus) during the Great Plague of London.

1667 Hook Head lighthouse in Co Wexford, Ireland is re-established. It is the oldest intact operational lighthouse in the world.

1667 The first use of the word 'Pandemonium' (the capital of Hell) appears in John Milton's *Paradise Lost*.

1667 Jean Baptiste Denys, physician to Louis XIV, performs the first human blood transfusion by transfusing the blood of a lamb to a 15-year old boy.

1667 French tapestry is established at the Gobelins Manufactory in Paris under the supervision of the royal painter, director and chief designer Charles Le Brun.

1669 The Chinese herbal medicine company Tongrentang is established in Beijing - now the largest producer of traditional Chinese medicine.

1669 Jan Swammerdam publishes *Historia Insectorum Generalis* in the Netherlands, explaining the process of metamorphosis in insects.

1669   Antonio Stradivari makes his
        first violin.

1670   The French colonize the
        island of Gorée near Dakar
        in modern Senegal.

1670 William Penn and William Mead are tried in London for preaching a Quaker sermon.

1671 The Académie royale d'architecture is founded by Louis XIV, the world's first school of architecture.

1671 The Observatoire de Paris – the world's first such national institution – is completed.

1672 Thomas Willis publishes the first English work on medical psychology, *Two Discourses concerning The Soul of Brutes, Which is that of the Vital and Sensitive of Man.*

1673 Antonio van Leewenhook uses powerful lenses to build microscopes and observes bee mouth parts and stings. Two years later he is the executor of Jan Vermeer's will.

1673 Leopold I, Spain, Netherlands and the Lutherans form an anti-French covenant.

1674 Father Jacques Marquette founds a mission on the shores of Lake Michigan to minister to the Illinois people. The mission will later grow into the city of Chicago.

1675 Gottfried Leibniz uses integral calculus for the first time to find the area under the graph of a function $y = f(x)$.

1675 Construction of the Royal Greenwich Observatory begins.

1675 The British Parliament orders the closure of all coffee houses as it is thought that they are centres of malicious gossip about the Government. The order is later reduced to a warning.

1679   The Habeas Corpus Act
        is passed in England.

c1680 The Byerley Turk thoroughbred horse is brought to England.

c1680 The Dodo (*Raphus cucullatus*), a flightless bird living on the island of Mauritius, becomes extinct.

1677 Jean Racine's tragedy *Phèdre* is first performed.

1675 A few days after the death of his beloved wife, the Japanese poet Saikaku composes a thousand-verse haikai poem over a period of about twelve hours.

1678 Robert Hooke publishes the Law of Elasticity including the solution to his Latin anagram on the concept ceiiinosssttuv, which translates as ut tensio, sic vis (as the extension, so the force).

1678 Elena Piscopia becomes the first woman to be awarded a university degree (in Philosophy) from the University of Padua.

1676 Antonie van Leeuwenhoek's credibility with the Royal Society is questioned when he sends a copy of his first observations of microscopic single-celled organisms.

1679 Excavation begins on the Malpas Tunnel on the Canal du Midi in Hérault in France which will become Europe's first navigable canal tunnel.

1676 Part of a dinosaur bone is recovered from a limestone quarry. Robert Plot, who later becomes the first keeper of the Ashmolean Museum in Oxford, concludes that it is the thigh bone of a giant human.

1677 *Ethics* by Benedict Spinoza is published posthumously – a work which opposes Descartes's mind–body dualism.

1676 Ole Rømer makes the first quantitative measurements of the speed of light, showing that light has a finite speed and does not travel instantaneously.

1680   LA MAISON DE MOLIÈRE IS FOUNDED IN PARIS NOW KNOWN AS COMÉDIE-FRANÇAISE.

1680   PUEBLO INDIANS CAPTURE SANTA FE (NEW MEXICO) FROM THE SPANISH.

1681   A LONDON WOMAN IS PUBLICLY FLOGGED FOR THE CRIME OF 'INVOLVING HERSELF IN POLITICS'.

1682   JAPANESE POET SAIKAKU WRITES THE FIRST OF MANY NOVELS THE LIFE OF AN AMOROUS MAN.

1682   SOPHIA ALEKSEYEVNA ALLIES HERSELF WITH A POWERFUL COURTIER AND POLITICIAN, PRINCE VASILY GALITZINE, AND INSTALLS HERSELF AS REGENT OF RUSSIA DURING THE MINORITY OF HER BROTHERS, PETER THE GREAT AND IVAN V.

1682   LOUIS XIV MOVES HIS COURT TO VERSAILLES.

1683   WILD BOARS ARE HUNTED TO EXTINCTION IN BRITAIN.

1684   GOTTFRIED LEIBNIZ PUBLISHES THE FIRST ACCOUNT OF DIFFERENTIAL CALCULUS.

1684   JAMES CHIPPERFIELD INTRODUCES PERFORMING ANIMALS AT THE FROST FAIRS BEING HELD ON THE FROZEN RIVER THAMES IN ENGLAND.

1684   IN ENGLAND SMUGGLED TEA IS DRUNK IN FAR GREATER QUANTITIES THAN LEGALLY IMPORTED TEA.

1685   FLEEING FROM JAMAICA AFTER BEING CHARGED WITH MURDER, ADAM BALDRIDGE FOUNDS A PIRATE BASE AT ÎLE SAINTE-MARIE IN MADAGASCAR

1685   SIMON USHAKOV PAINTS THE LAST SUPPER.

1685   The revocation of the Edict of Nantes
       by Louis XIV forces 400,000 Hugenots
       to leave France.

1685   The first street lighting is introduced
       in London with oil lamps to be lit
       outside every tenth house on moonless
       winter nights.

1685   Charles Allen publishes the first book
       in English on dentistry, *The Operator
       for the Teeth*.

1685   Johann Sebastian Bach is born.
       George Frideric Handel is born.

1687   Isaac Newton describes universal
       gravitation and the three laws of
       motion in *Philosophiae Naturalis
       Principia Mathematica*.

1687   An Ottoman Turk ammunition dump
       inside the Parthenon is ignited by
       Venetian bombardment causing
       severe damage to the building and
       its sculptures.

1688   Edward Lloyd opens the London coffee
       house that becomes a popular meeting
       place for shipowners, merchants,
       insurance brokers and underwriters,
       later known as 'Lloyds of London'.

1689   The Tsar of Russia decrees the
       construction of the Great Siberian
       Route to China.

1690   John Locke's publication *Two Treatises
       of Government* argues for government
       by popular consent.

1690   The newspaper *Publick Occurrences
       Both Forreign & Domestick* is first
       published in Massachusetts after which
       it is suppressed by colonial authorities.

1690   Hishikawa Moronobu creates Beauty
       looking back, a ukiyo-e woodblock print.

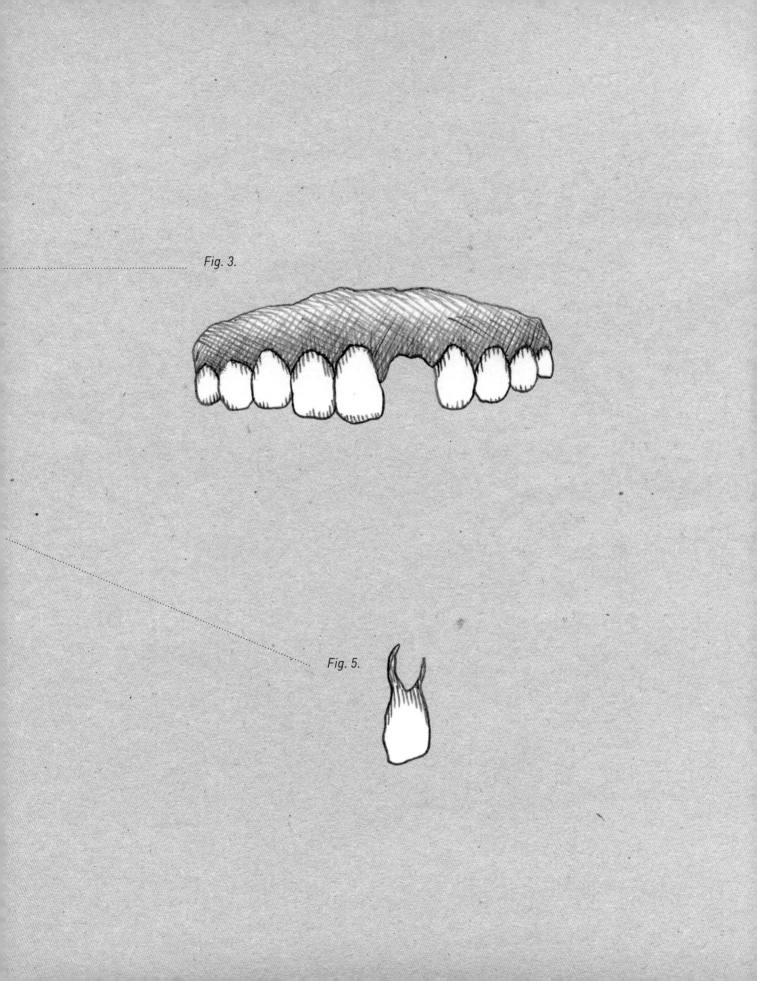

Fig. 3.

Fig. 5.

1690 – 1695

1691 EDMOND HALLEY completes plans for a DIVING BELL capable of remaining submerged for extended periods of time.

1690 *Denis Papin builds a model of a* **PISTON STEAM ENGINE***, the first of its kind.*

1692

THE Salem

begin in Salem Village, Massachusetts Bay Colony,

1690 Earliest recorded sighting of the planet Uranus by John Flamsteed, the first Astronomer Royal in England, who mistakenly catalogues it as the star 34 Tauri.

1693 China concentrates all its foreign trade in *CANTON* forbidding European ships to land anywhere else.

1690 *The Court Midwife by Justine Siegemund is published - the first German medical textbook to be written by a woman.*

1690 *The Battle of the Boyne.*

1690 *The* **CLARINET** *is invented in an evolution from an earlier instrument called the chalumeau, the first true single reed instrument.*

Ditch TRIALS

with the charging of three women with WITCHCRAFT.

1693 John Banks' historical play ***THE INNOCENT USURPER***, about Lady Jane Grey, is banned from the stage.

1694 THE BANK OF ENGLAND *is founded to act as the government's banker and debt-manager*

c1694 JOHANN PACHELBEL *composes* CANON IN D

SIXTEEN N

1695 In Amsterdam, the bank Wed. Jean Deutz & Sn. floats the first sovereign bonds on the local market, issued for 12 years bearing 5% interest. The scheme is designed to fund a 1.5 million guilders loan to the Holy Roman Emperor.

1695 English pirate Henry Every captures the Grand Mughal ship *Ganj-i-Sawai*, one of the most profitable raids in history. In response, Emperor Aurangzeb threatens to put an end to all English trading in India.

1695 Johann Sebastian Bach is orphaned and taken in by his cousin Johann Christoph Bach.

1695 A window tax is imposed in England and some windows are bricked up to avoid the tax. The same year a £2 fine is imposed for swearing.

1696 A famine wipes out almost a third of the population of Finland and a fifth of the population of Estonia.

1697 Antonio Stradivari makes the 'Castelbarco' cello and the following year the 'Cabriac' violin.

FINE IS M

SWEARING

1697 French writer Charles Perrault publishes a collection of then-popular fairy tales, including *Red Riding Hood* and *The Sleeping Beauty*.

1697 The earliest known first-class cricket match takes place in Sussex.

1698 Tsar Peter I of Russia imposes a tax on beards: all men except priests and peasants are required to pay a tax of 100 rubles a year while commoners are required to pay one kopeck each.

1699 Isaac Newton is appointed as Master of the Mint.

1700 The death of Carlos II marks the end of the Hapsburg line in Spain.

1700 Russia begins numbering its calendar from the birth of Christ (Anno Domini) instead of since the Creation (Anno Mundi).

1704 Newton publishes Opticks describing how
light can be split into a spectrum of different colours.

1705 Edmond Halley notes that the (
1703 The ritual suicide
1701 Jethro Tull invents a horse-drawn dril
1701 The
1700 An inventory made for the Medici fami
1702 Guillaume Amo
1700 William Penn, founder of the f

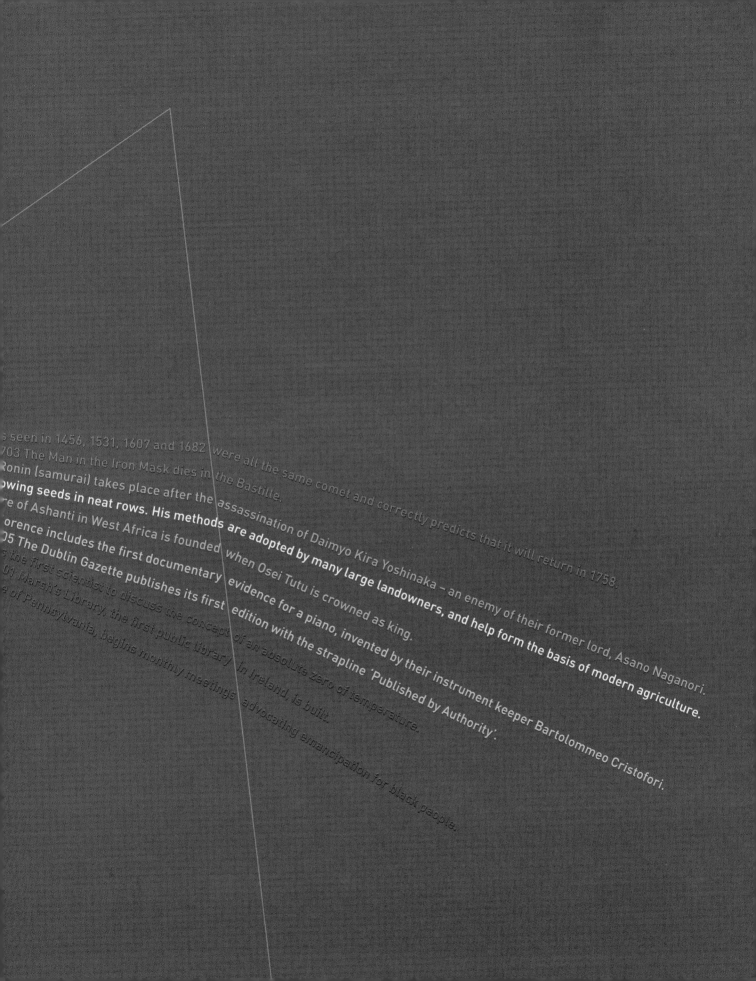

...s seen in 1456, 1531, 1607 and 1682 were all the same comet and correctly predicts that it will return in 1758.

...703 The Man in the Iron Mask dies in the Bastille.

...Ronin (samurai) takes place after the assassination of Daimyo Kira Yoshinaka – an enemy of their former lord, Asano Naganori.

...owing seeds in neat rows. His methods are adopted by many large landowners, and help form the basis of modern agriculture.

...e of Ashanti in West Africa is founded when Osei Tutu is crowned as king.

...orence includes the first documentary evidence for a piano, invented by their instrument keeper Bartolommeo Cristofori.

...05 The Dublin Gazette publishes its first edition with the strapline 'Published by Authority'.

...the first scientist to discuss the concept of an absolute zero of temperature.

...01 Marsh's Library), the first public library, in Ireland, is built.

...e of Pennsylvania, begins monthly meetings advocating emancipation for black people.

1705 The Venetian painter Rosalba Carriera becomes the first woman to be elected to the Accademia di San Luca in Rome.

1706 Thomas Twining opens the first tea-room in Europe, located at 216 Strand, London.

1706 William Jones proposes using the symbol π to represent the ratio of the circumference of a circle to its diameter.

1707 Mount Fuji begins to erupt in Japan.

1708 Calcareous hard-paste porcelain is produced for the first time in Europe at Dresden.

1709 Alexander Selkirk is rescued from shipwreck on a desert island, inspiring the book Robinson Crusoe by Daniel Defoe.

1709 Europe's coldest period in 500 years begins with parts of the Atlantic coast and the river Seine freezing – occurring during the time of low sun spot activity known as the Maunder Minimum.

1709 A collapsible umbrella is introduced in Paris.

1710 Jakob Christof Le Blon invents a three-colour printing process with red, blue, and yellow ink. He later adds black introducing the earliest four-colour printing process.

c1710 Antonio Vivaldi composes Nulla in mundo pax sincera.

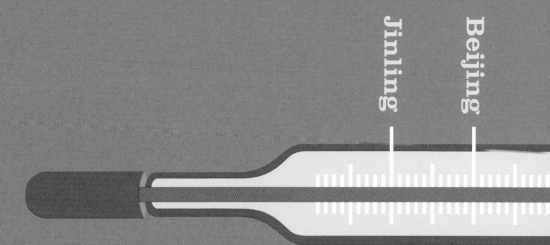

Jinling

Beijing

1710 Alexis Littré is the first physician to suggest the possibility of performing a colostomy for obstruction of the colon.

1710 Beijing becomes the most populated city of the world, taking the lead from Constantinople (Istanbul).

1710 Ten ships leave London for the New York colony, carrying over 4,000 people.

1710 The world's first copyright legislation is introduced: Britain's *Statute of Anne*.

1711 The first Mardi Gras parade called Boeuf Gras (fatted ox) is held in Mobile, Alabama with 16 men pushing a large papier-mâché ox head on a cart.

1711 The 'calculus controversy' erupts - an argument between mathematicians Isaac Newton and Gottfried Leibniz over who had first invented calculus.

Constantinople

Beijing

1710
—
1715

1712 A Newcomen steam engine is built to pump water out of mines in the Black Country of England, the first practical device to harness the power of steam to produce mechanical work.

1712 Arcangelo Corelli's *Concerti Grossi* are first performed.

1713 *Cato, a Tragedy* by Joseph Addison (with a prologue by Alexander Pope) is first performed.

1713 *Ars Conjectandi* (The Art of Conjecturing) by Jakob Bernoulli lays the foundation for probability theory.

1714 The British parliament votes to offer a reward 'for such person or persons as shall discover the Longitude.'

1714 Daniel Farenheit improves on Galileo's thermometer by sealing the mercury in glass.

1715 The first fire extinguisher is invented.

1716 A sculpture park is established in the Summer Garden (Letni Sad) at Saint Petersburg.

1716 America's first lighthouse, Boston Light, is built.

1716 The Kangxi Dictionary is published in China, laying the foundation for most references to Han characters studied today.

1717 Handel's *Water Music* premières on the river Thames based on a request from King George I. The concert is performed by 50 musicians playing on a barge near the royal barge from which the King listens with close friends.

1717 François Marie Arouet is sentenced to imprisonment in the Bastille because of his satirical verse about the Regent of France. While there he writes his first literary work, *Œdipe*, using his adopted pen name, Voltaire.

1718 The Charitable Infirmary in Dublin is founded by six surgeons in Ireland and becomes the first public voluntary hospital in the British Isles.

1718 Blackbeard, the pirate, is killed in action at Ocracoke Inlet in North Carolina, after receiving five musketball wounds and twenty sword lacerations.

1719 The Principality of Liechtenstein is created within the Holy Roman Empire.

1719 *Robinson Crusoe* by Daniel Defoe is published.

1719 Prussia conducts the first systematic census in Europe.

1720 The Great Plague of Marseille is the last major outbreak of bubonic plague in Europe.

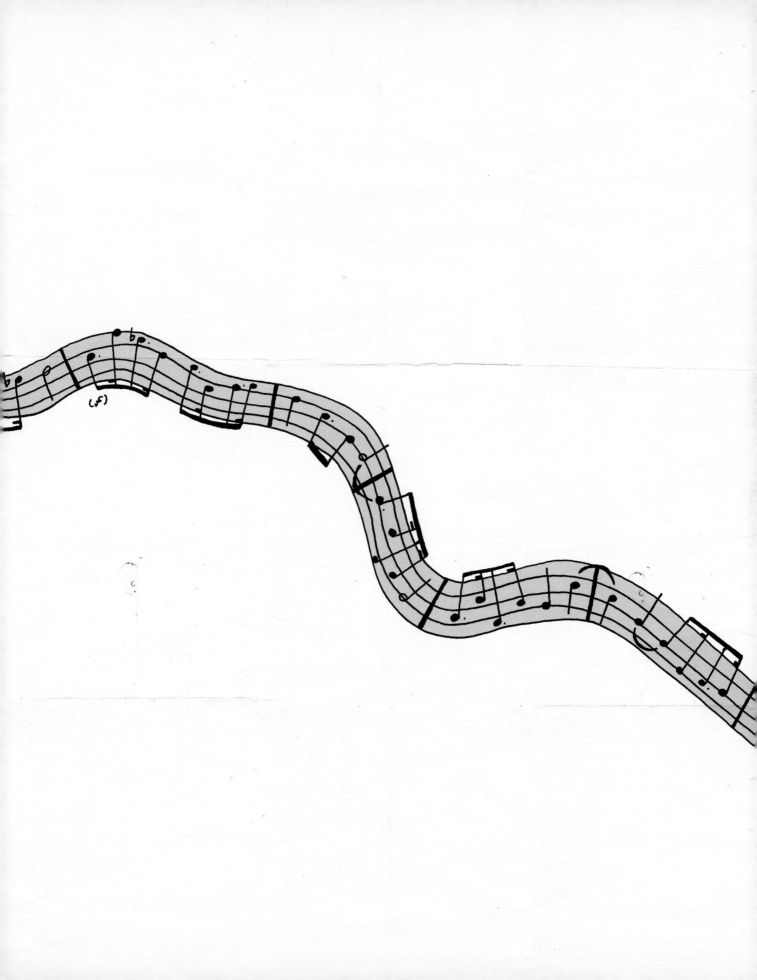

1720   J S Bach composes *Air on a G string*.

1720   The development of the post-chaise in France hugely increases the ease of travel overland and ushers in the era of 'The Grand Tour'.

1720   The first yacht club in the world, the Royal Cork Yacht Club, is founded in Ireland.

1722   The Safavids Persian dynasty ends. At the height of their power they controlled all of modern Iran, Azerbaijan and Armenia, most of Iraq, Georgia, Afghanistan and the Caucasus, as well as parts of Pakistan, Tajikistan and Turkey.

1722   At the age of 16 Benjamin Franklin adopts the pseudonym 'Mrs Silence Dogood', a middle-aged widow, in order to publish letters in *The New-England Courant*.

1722   Abraham de Moivre's formula connects complex numbers and trigonometry.

1723   Love suicides in Japan (Shinjū) reach their peak during the Edo period.

1723   Antonio Vivaldi composes *The Four Seasons*.

1724   Daniel Bernouilli expresses the numbers of the Fibonacci sequence in terms of the golden ratio.

1724   *Peter the Wild Boy*, a feral child, is found near Helpensen in Hanover, Germany.

1725   Navigator Vitus Bering is sent by Peter the Great to explore the North Pacific for potential colonization. The abundance of fur-bearing mammals on the Alaskan coast attracts Russian interest as overhunting has depleted Siberian stocks.

1727 Euler uses the notation e in connection with the theory of natural logarithms, also known as Euler's number.

1727 An elderly woman known as Jenny Horne becomes the last alleged witch in the British Isles to be executed when she is burned at the stake in Dornoch, Scotland.

INDIA

LAPUTA

1725 The binary numeral system is invented by Basile Bouchon.

1726 Jonathan Swift writes *Gulliver's Travels*.

1727 Billiards becomes so popular that it is played in almost every café in Paris.

1727 Coffee plantations are established in Brazil.

1729 *The Bayeux Tapestry* is re-discovered by scholars during its annual display in Bayeux Cathedral. Nearly 70 metres long, it depicts the events that led up to the Norman conquest of England culminating in the Battle of Hastings in 1066.

1725 Catherine I becomes the first female Empress of Russia after the death of her husband Peter the Great. They had married secretly in 1707 and had twelve children, only two of whom survived into adulthood.

1727 Construction begins on the Jantar Mantar in Jaipur, a collection of architectural astronomical instruments commissioned by Maharaja Jai Singh II.

sun

1727 Benjamin Franklin founds the *Junto*, a group of 'like minded aspiring artisans and tradesmen who hope to improve themselves while they improve their community.' From this group Franklin conceives the idea of a subscription library.

1725 The first meeting of a Masonic Grand Lodge of Ireland is held in Dublin.

ELEVATION

1733 The perambulator is invented by architect William Kent for the children of the 3rd Duke of Devonshire.

45°

DETAIL

1.

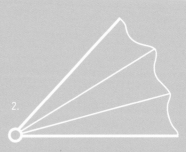

2.

PLAN

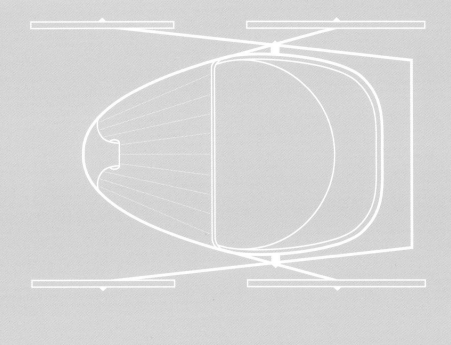

NOTES

1730 *The Beggar's Opera* which lampoons the Italian opera style, is so popular that a deck of playing cards based on the characters is printed.

1731 Laura Bassi becomes the first official female university teacher on being appointed Professor of Anatomy at the University of Bologna at the age of 21.

1731 Marie Angelique, a feral child (later known as The Maid of Châlons) is discovered in Songy in Champagne, France.

1731 The orrery is invented as an apparatus to show the relative positions of heavenly bodies in the solar system by using balls moved by wheelwork.

1731 Johann Scheuchzer's *Physica Sacra*, which attempts to provide a scientific explanation of Biblical history, is published.

1732 Canaletto paints *View of the Entrance to the Arsenale di Venezia.*

1732 Philip Miller of the Chelsea Physic Garden sends cotton seeds to Georgia, America.

1733 The flying shuttle loom is patented, enabling faster weaving and increasing demand for yarn.

1733 De Moivre publishes work on the normal curve as an approximation of the Binomial distribution.

1735 The first successful appendectomy is performed by French surgeon Claudius Aymand in London.

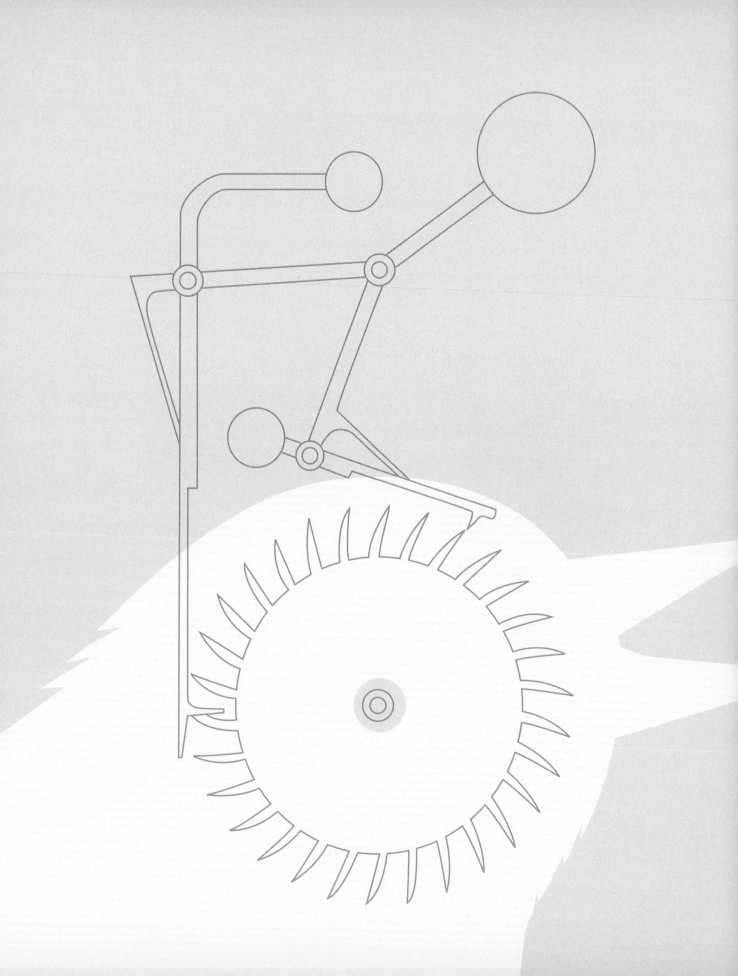

1735 John Harrison invents the first of his marine chronometers, which enables sailors to calculate their longitude with accuracy.

1735 Charles Marie de La Condamine leads an expedition of French scientists to Peru to try to calculate the circumference of the earth.

1735 Leonhard Euler solves the problem of the seven bridges of Königsberg, laying down the foundations of graph theory and prefiguring the concept of topology.

1735 Carl Linnaeus publishes his classification system *Systema Naturae*. The philosopher Rousseau sends him the message, 'tell him I know no greater man on earth'.

1737 The oldest existing English language daily newspaper in the world, *The Belfast News Letter*, is founded in Ireland.

1737 *Il Newtonianismo per le Dame* by Francesco Algarotti is published. A translation by Elizabeth Carter is published two years later under the title *Sir Isaac Newton's Philosophy Explain'd for the Use of the Ladies*.

1738 Franz Ketterer invents the cuckoo clock.

1738 A collection of essays, *Propositiones Philosophicae* by the mathematician Maria Gaetana Agnesi is published. Many of the essays include her conviction that women should be educated.

1738 Bernoulli's principle is published in *Hydrodynamica*.

1740 Anna Ivanovna, Empress of Russia, arranges a marriage for Prince Galitzine who has displeased her. She forces him to spend his wedding night with his bride in an elaborate ice palace, complete with ice bed, ice furniture and ice sculptures.

1740 Charles VI, Holy Roman Emperor dies after consuming death cap mushrooms.

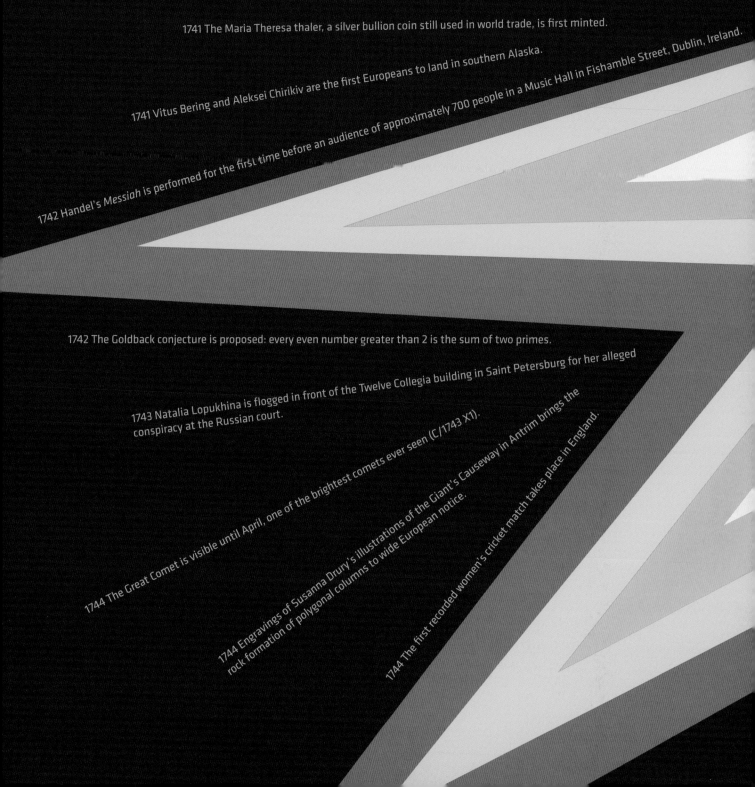

1740 The reign of Frederick the Great, Frederick II King of Prussia begins.

1741 The Maria Theresa thaler, a silver bullion coin still used in world trade, is first minted.

1741 Vitus Bering and Aleksei Chirikiv are the first Europeans to land in southern Alaska.

1742 Handel's Messiah is performed for the first time before an audience of approximately 700 people in a Music Hall in Fishamble Street, Dublin, Ireland.

1742 The Goldback conjecture is proposed: every even number greater than 2 is the sum of two primes.

1743 Natalia Lopukhina is flogged in front of the Twelve Collegia building in Saint Petersburg for her alleged conspiracy at the Russian court.

1744 The Great Comet is visible until April, one of the brightest comets ever seen (C/1743 X1).

1744 Engravings of Susanna Drury's illustrations of the Giant's Causeway in Antrim brings the rock formation of polygonal columns to wide European notice.

1744 The first recorded women's cricket match takes place in England.

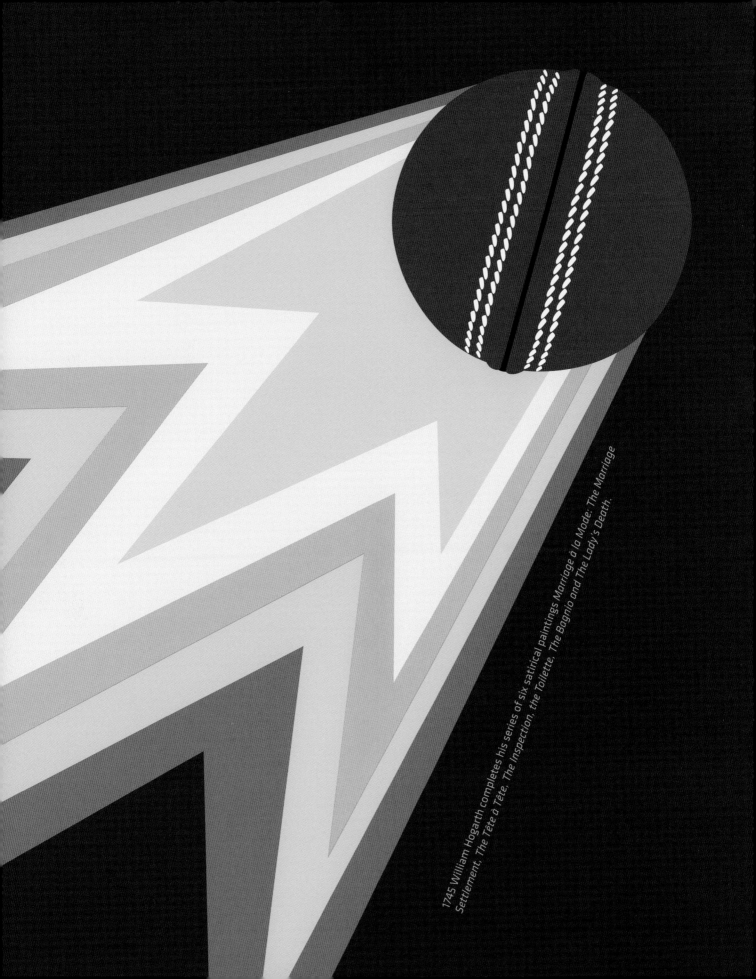

1745 William Hogarth completes his series of six satirical paintings Marriage à la Mode: The Marriage Settlement, The Tête à Tête, The Inspection, the Toilette, The Bagnio and The Lady's Death.

1745 The Company of Surgeons separates from the Company of Barbers of London.

1745 Pieter van Musschenbroek invents the Leyden jar, a device for storing electric charge - the first capacitor.

1746 The Dress Act comes into force making the wearing of 'the Highland Dress', including tartan or a kilt, illegal in Scotland.

1747 A tribal council of native Pashtun people creates modern Afghanistan and Ahmad Shah Durrani becomes King.

1747 In one of the first controlled trials, James Lind shows that the eating of citrus fruits prevents scurvy.

1748 Eva Ekeblad becomes the first female member of the Royal Swedish Academy of Sciences.

1748 The first comprehensive excavation of Pompeii begins.

1748 Lewis Paul invents a machine for carding - a mechanical process that separates fibres and assembles them into a loose strand suitable for spinning and weaving.

1748 The Kabuki drama *Chūshingura*, based on the revenge suicide by 47 Ronin (samurai), is performed.

1748 Montesquieu advocates the separation of powers in *The Spirit of the Laws*.

1749 The first official performance of George Frideric Handel's *Music for the Royal Fireworks* finishes early due to the outbreak of fire.

1749 Denis Diderot writes Lettre sur les aveugles à l'usage de ceux qui voient (Letter on the Blind For the Use of Those Who See). The subject is a discussion of the interrelation between man's reason and the knowledge acquired through perception of the five senses.

1751 Robert Whytt discovers the nature of the pupillary reflex, the contraction of the pupil in response to light, later known as Whytt's reflex.

1752 The Khan As'ad Pasha in Damascus is completed.

1750 Hannah Snell, a British woman who had disguised herself as a man to become a soldier, reveals her sex to her Royal Marines compatriots.

1754 *Discourse on the Origin and Basis of Inequality Among Men* is written by philosopher Jean-Jacques Rousseau in response to an essay competition: *What is the origin of inequality among men, and is it authorized by natural law?*

1750 Galley slavery is abolished in Europe.

1752 The Tiergarten Schönbrunn is established in Vienna - the world's oldest zoo.

1753 Old Blush, a China rose derived from *Rosa chinensis*, is the first East Asian rose to reach Europe.

1752 The world's first steeplechase is held as the result of a wager between Cornelius O'Callaghan and Edmund Blake who race four miles cross-country from Buttevant Church to St. Leger Church in Doneraile, Cork, Ireland.

1752 Benjamin Franklin flies a kite during a thunderstorm and demonstrates that lightning is an electrical discharge.

1750 Riots break out in Paris, fuelled by rumours of police abducting children.

1752 The Gregorian calendar is adopted by England and its colonies 170 years after the first countries made the changeover.

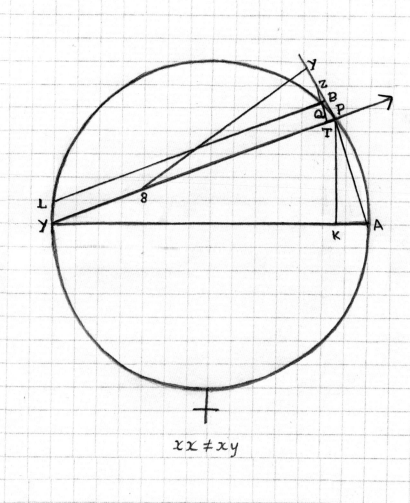

$$xx \neq xy$$

1759   Emilie du Châtelet's translation and commentary on Newton's 'Principia Mathematica' is published posthumously. Voltaire, one of her lovers, declared in a letter to his friend, King Frederick II of Prussia, that du Châtelet was 'a great man whose only fault was being a woman'.

1755	Franz Joseph Haydn composes his first string quartet.
c1755	Joseph Black discovers 'fixed air' now known as carbon dioxide.
1755	Leopold Mozart composes Divertimento in F major "Musical Sleigh Ride"
1756	St. Patrick's Day is celebrated in New York City for the first time, at the Crown and Thistle Tavern.
1756	The Marine Society is founded in London, the world's oldest seafarers' charity.
1756	François Boucher paints portraits of Madame de Pompador.
1757	A Philosophical Enquiry into the Origin of Our Ideas of the Sublime and Beautiful by Edmund Burke is published.
1759	The Royal Botanic Gardens at Kew in London are founded.
1760	Western countries pay 3,000,000 ounces of silver for Chinese goods.
1760	Dr James Fordyce's two-volume compendium Sermons for Young Women is published.

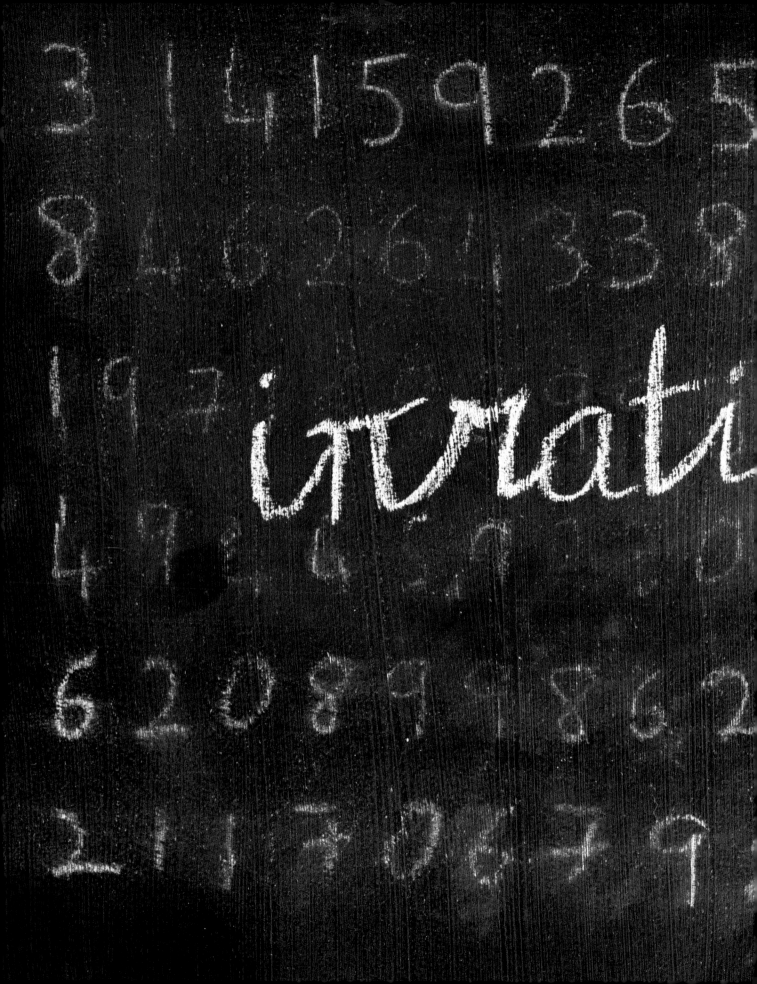

1761 Johann Heinrich Lambert proves that π is irrational.

1761 The theory of latent heat proposed by Joseph Black marks the beginning of thermodynamics.

1761 Astronomers from Britain, France, Sweden and Russia set up telescopes across the globe to time the transit of Venus across the Sun and thus calculate the distance between the Earth and the Sun.

1761 The first veterinary school in the world is created in Lyon by equerry Claude Bourgelat.

1762 Kobayashi Issa is born. He becomes one of the four great haiku masters with Bashō (b1644), Buson (b1716) and Shiki (b1867).

1762 The Society for Equitable Assurances on Lives and Survivorships is established in London, pioneering mutual insurance using actuarial science.

1762 The Trevi Fountain in Rome is completed after thirty years.

1762 Construction starts on the Petit Trianon, a small château at Versailles, commissioned by Louis XV for his mistress, Madame de Pompadour.

1762 Rousseau's concept of the 'noble savage' appears in his publication Of The Social Contract, Or Principles of Political Right.

1764 The spinning jenny, a multi-spool spinning wheel, is invented by James Hargreaves.

1764 Cesare Beccaria writes On Crime and Punishment, a work which includes the condemnation of torture and the death penalty.

1764 The first state-financed higher education institution for women in Europe is ordered by decree under Catherine the Great, Empress of Russia.

World Map

JIGSAW

1767 John Spilsbury makes the first jigsaw puzzle. He intends to teach geography by cutting maps into pieces but soon jigsaws are made for entertainment.

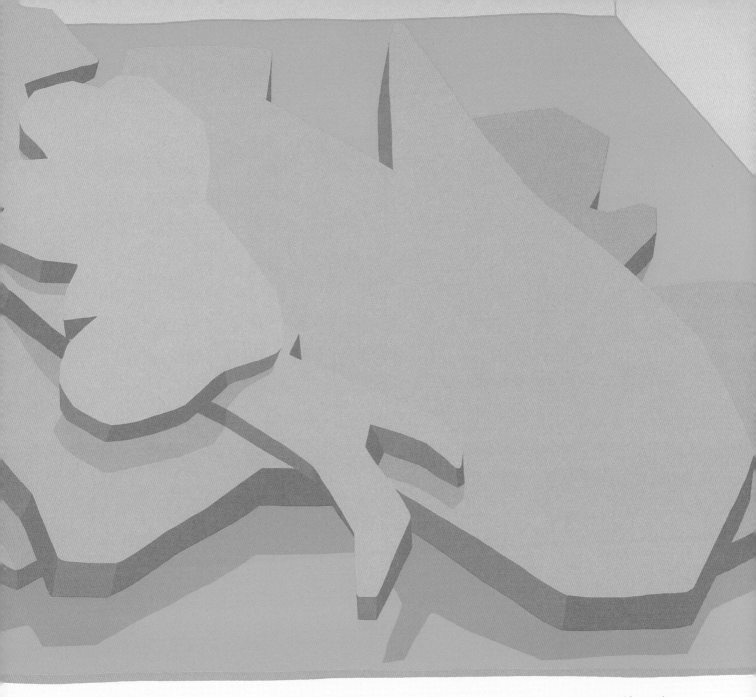

1765 James Watt makes a breakthrough in the development of the steam engine by constructing a model with a separate condenser.

1765 Beginning of Sturm und Drang (Storm and Urge) - a free expression movement in German literature and music.

1766 Henry Cavendish discovers hydrogen which he calls 'inflammable air' noted in his paper On Factitious Airs. Antoine Lavoisier later reproduces Cavendish's experiment and gives the element its name.

1767 The Nautical Almanac published by the Royal Greenwich Observatory gives mariners the means to find their longitude while at sea using tables of lunar distances.

1768 Bougainvillea is first classified in Brazil by Philibert Commerçon.

1768 Joseph Wright of Derby paints An Experiment on a Bird in the Air Pump. The painting depicts a natural philosopher recreating one of Robert Boyle's air pump experiments, in which a bird is deprived of air, before a group of onlookers.

1768 Si Dieu n'existait pas, il faudrait l'inventer (If God did not exist, it would be necessary to invent him), Voltaire.

1768 Corsica is sold to France by the Republic of Genoa. Napoleon Bonaparte is born on the island the following year.

1769 Captain Cook observes the Transit of Venus from Tahiti at a location still known as Point Venus.

1770 Captain Cook and the crew of the Endeavour land in Botany Bay.

1773 In protest against the tax policy of the British government, colonists board ships in Boston harbour and throw the cargo of tea into the sea – The Boston Tea Party.

1774 Joseph Priestley isolates oxygen in the form of a gas which he calls 'dephlogisticated air'.

1771 Jean-Baptiste-Siméon Chardin paints Autoportrait aux Besicles.

1774 Empress Maria Theresa of Austria develops the first state education system, The General School for Boys.

1774 Joseph Priestley isolates oxygen in the form of a gas, which he calls "dephlogisticated air".

1775 The American Revolution.

1773 The East India Company starts operations in Bengal to smuggle opium into China.

1771 Luigi Boccherini composes String Quintet in E.

1772 The Art of War, a Chinese military treatise written during the Warring States period (476BC – 221BC), is translated into French by the Jesuit Jean Joseph Marie Amiot.

1772 The partition of Poland marks the end of the Polish– Lithuanian Commonwealth.

1773 John Harrison receives the Longitude prize for his invention of the first marine chronometer.

1775
-
1780

1775 On his second voyage, Captain Cook uses a marine chronometer (a copy of John Harrison's H4 clock) to measure longitude. *Resolution* is the first ship known to cross the Antarctic Circle.

1775 Catherine the Great gives the nobles absolute control over their serfs.

1776 In his publication, *The Wealth of Nations*, Adam Smith warns of the 'collusive nature of business interests, which may form cabals or monopolies, fixing the highest price which can be squeezed out of the buyers'.

1776 United States Declaration of Independence.

1776 The Bavarian Illuminati is founded by Adam Weishaupt with an initial membership of five.

1777 The Code Duello is adopted by the gentlemen of counties Tipperary, Galway, Mayo, Sligo and Roscommon in Ireland as 'the form' for pistol duels. It becomes widely adopted throughout the English-speaking world.

1777 Morocco becomes the first nation to formally recognize the American colonies.

c1777 Francisco Goya paints *The Parasol*.

1778 The Tây Sơn Dynasty is established in Vietnam.

1778 The term 'thoroughbred' is first used in the United States in an advertisement in a Kentucky gazette to describe a New Jersey stallion called Pilgarlick.

1779 An iron bridge is erected across the River Severn in England, the world's first bridge built entirely of cast iron.

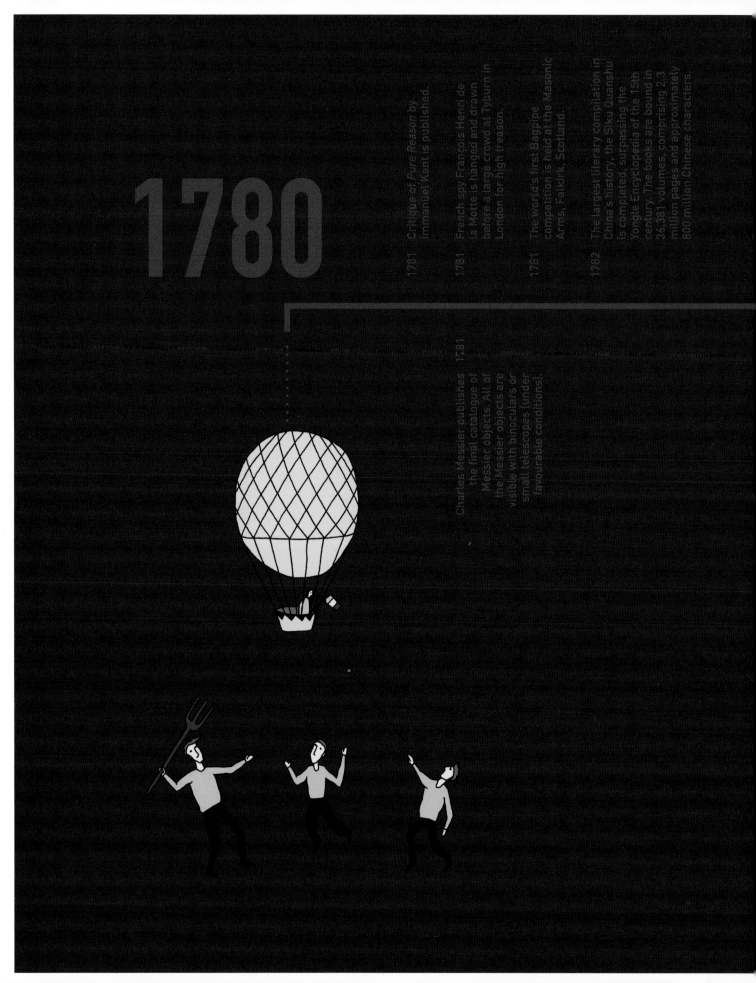

1780

1785

1782 The bald eagle is chosen as the emblem of the United States of America.

1783 Ireland's last grey wolf is killed.

1783 The first manned hot-air balloon, designed by the Montgolfier brothers, takes off from the Bois de Boulogne.

1784 Explorer Grigory Shelekhov founds Russia's first permanent settlement in Alaska at Three Saints Bay.

1785 A hot air balloon crashes in Tullamore, Ireland, causing a fire that burns down about 100 houses, making it the world's first aviation disaster.

1782 In Switzerland, Anna Göldi is the last person in the world to be legally sentenced to death for witchcraft.

c1784 Queen Marie Antoinette is implicated in participating in a crime to defraud the crown jewellers of the cost of a diamond necklace.

1786 Tuscany is the first European state to abolish the death penalty.

1787 Antonio Canova's statue Psyche Revived by Cupid's Kiss is commissioned.

1787 HMS Bounty sets sail for the South Seas under Captain William Bligh.

1789 The Bill of Rights: the first ten amendments to the American constitution.

1789 George Washington is elected as the first President of the United States.

1785 Friedrich Schiller writes Ode to Joy, a poem on which the closing choral section of Beethoven's Ninth Symphony (1824) is based.

1789 Jeremy Bentham, the founder of modern utilitarianism, argues that all punishment in itself is evil: it ought only to be admitted in as far as it promises to exclude some greater evil. John Stuart Mill will later become Bentham's student.

1789 George Washington is elected as the first President of the United States.

1789 Storming of the Bastille, 14th July. The prison contains just seven inmates at the time of its storming.

1787 Mozart's Don Giovanni is first performed in the Estates Theatre in Prague.

1789 Giacomo Casanova starts writing Histoire de ma vie (Story of my Life).

1789 Aboriginal Woollarawarre Bennelong is kidnapped and brought to the settlement at Sydney Cove to act as interlocutor between the British and the Eora people.

1792 Mary Wollston

1794 The French revolutiona

1791 Wolfgang Amadeus Mozart composes The Magic Flute a

1793 Jacques–Louis David paint

1794 Erasmus Darwin, grandfather of C
including arguments that all extant org

1795 The British Royal Navy makes the use of lemon juice mand

1791 Olympe de Gouges publishes Déclaration des droits de la femme et e

1792 The city of Freetown in Sierra Leone is fo

1791 Toussaint Breda (Louverture) leads a slave rebellion in the French colony of Saint Domingue on Hispaniola.

1791 Luigi Galvani publishes his discoveries in animal electricity, later known as Galvanism.

...ites A Vindication of the Rights of Woman. Her daughter, born five years later, is Mary Shelley, author of Frankenstein.

...rnment under the leadership of Maximilien Robespierre votes for the abolition of slavery.

...Clarinet Concerto. He dies at the age of 35 leaving the unfinished Requiem in D Minor, his 626th composition.

...fort de Marat.

...Darwin, publishes Zoonomia, a medical work

...s are descended from one common ancestor.

...to prevent scurvy.

...itoyenne, Declaration of the Rights of Woman and the Female Citizen.

...by abolitionist John Clarkson as a land for freed African American slaves.

1791 Giovanni Battista Guglielmini demonstrates the rotation of the Earth in Bologna.

1796 Edward Jenner discovers that immunity to smallpox can be produced by inoculation with material from the cowpox virus, a process that will become known as vaccination.

1796 Jean Senebier demonstrates that green plants consume carbon dioxide and release oxygen under the influence of light.

c1796 Roulette (little wheel) is first played in Paris.

1797 Horatio Nelson is wounded at the Battle of Santa Cruz and loses his arm.

1797 The XYZ Affair is caused by an international incident in which the French Foreign Minister, Talleyrand, demands bribes and a loan in exchange for facilitating diplomatic negotiations between France and the United States.

1797 London haberdasher John Hetherington wears a top hat in public causing a near riot and is arrested for a breach of the peace.

1797 Joseph Haydn composes Gott erhalte Franz den Kaiser as an anthem for the birthday of the Austrian Emperor Francis II. The melody will later be used for the German national anthem.

1798 Samuel Taylor Coleridge writes The Rime of the Ancient Mariner.

1799 Jeanne Geneviève Labrosse becomes the first woman to jump from a balloon with a parachute, from an altitude of 900 meters.

1799 A 12-year-old boy, Conrad Reed, finds what he describes as a 'heavy yellow rock,' in Cabarrus County, North Carolina and makes it a doorstop in his home. The rock is discovered to be gold in 1802, initiating the first gold rush in the United States.

1799 Lithography is invented by the Austrian printer Alois Senefelder by using a matrix of fine-grained limestone.

1799 The Rosetta Stone, an ancient Egyptian stele inscribed with a decree issued at Memphis in 196 BC for King Ptolemy V, is discovered near the town of Rashid in the Nile Delta.

1796 Edward Jenner discovers that immunity to smallpox can be produced by inoculation with material from the cowpox virus, a process that will become known as vaccination.

1796 Jean Senebier demonstrates that green plants consume carbon dioxide and release oxygen under the influence of light.

c1796 Roulette (little wheel) is first played in Paris.

1797 Horatio Nelson is wounded at the Battle of Santa Cruz and loses his arm.

1797 The XYZ Affair is caused by an international incident in which the French Foreign Minister, Talleyrand, demands bribes and a loan in exchange for facilitating diplomatic negotiations between France and the United States.

1797 London haberdasher John Hetherington wears a top hat in public causing a near riot and is arrested for a breach of the peace.

1797 Joseph Haydn composes *Gott erhalte Franz den Kaiser* as an anthem for the birthday of the Austrian Emperor Francis II. The melody will later be used for the German national anthem.

1798 Samuel Taylor Coleridge writes *The Rime of the Ancyent Marinere*.

1799 Jeanne Geneviève Labrosse becomes the first woman to jump from a balloon with a parachute, from an altitude of 900 meters.

1799 A 12-year-old boy, Conrad Reed, finds what he describes as a 'heavy yellow rock' in Cabarrus County, North Carolina and makes it a doorstop in his home. The rock is discovered to be gold in 1802, initiating the first gold rush in the United States.

1799 Lithography is invented by the Austrian printer Alois Senefelder by using a matrix of fine-grained limestone.

1799 The Rosetta Stone, an ancient Egyptian stele inscribed with a decree issued at Memphis in 196 BC for King Ptolemy V, is discovered near the town of Rashid in the Nile Delta.

John Dalton begins using symbols to represent different elements and publishes Atomic Theory of the Elements the following year.

1803

Alexander Hamilton, one of the founding fathers of America, is shot during a duel with Vice President Aaron Burr and dies the next day.

1804

Thomas Young's double slit experiment demonstrates the wave form of light.

1803

Alessandro Volta invents the voltaic pile, an early electric battery, which produces a steady electric current.

1800

The first asteroid is discovered and named Ceres.

1801

As the result of a professional disagreement over the 'galvanic response' tabled by Galvani, Indonesia's independence 149 years later. The islands of Indonesia are known as the Dutch East Indies until

1800

The Dutch East India Company goes bankrupt.

1801

Ultraviolet radiation is discovered by Johann Wilhelm Ritter.

1803   Irish rebel Robert Emmet makes a speech from the dock, on the eve of his execution for high treason, with the closing words, 'When my country takes her place among the nations of the earth, then and not till then, let my epitaph be written. I have done.'

1804   Haiti gains independence from France and becomes the first black republic as a result of the successful slave revolt.

1801   Elgin's agents start to remove many of the surviving sculptures from the Parthenon, Propylaea, and Erechtheum.

1805   Mohammad Ali Pasha becomes the self-declared Khedive (Governor) of Egypt and Sudan.

1805 The Battle of Trafalgar. 1805 *Conversations on Chemistry* by Jane Marcet is published anonymously. It becomes one of the first elementary science textbooks and provides inspiration for the young Michael Faraday. 1805 The Horse Patrol, a mounted law enforcement force, is founded in London. 1806 The abdication of Francis II brings the Holy Roman Empire to an end after almost a millennium. 1807 The *Clermont* leaves New York City for Albany on the Hudson River, inaugurating the first commercial steamboat service in the world. 1807 The world's oldest international football stadium, the Racecourse Ground, opens in Wales, although it will not host football games until 1872. 1807 Pall Mall in London is the first street to be lit by gas. 1808 In Vienna Ludwig van Beethoven conducts the première of his *Fifth Symphony*, *Sixth Symphony*, *Fourth Piano Concerto* and *Choral Fantasy*. 1808 Johann Wolfgang von Goethe publishes *Faust*. 1808 The *Smolny Institute for Noble Maidens* is is established in St Petersburg - the first state-financed higher education institution for women in Europe. 1809 The wearing of masks at balls is forbidden in Boston, Massachusetts. 1809 Charles Darwin and Abraham Lincoln are both born on 12th February.

1810 A pioneering study of the localization of mental functions in the brain is published popularizing the study of phrenology.

1814 Missionaries in New Zealand make the first attempts to write down the Māori language.

1810 The marriage of Napoleon and Josephine is annulled and Napoleon marries Marie-Louise of Austria.

1810 Bernardo O'Higgins Riquelme joins the revolt against the French-dominated Spanish government in Chile. He is later known as one of the founding fathers of Chile.

1812 Laplace's Demon – an essay on a deterministic world – is published: 'Given the precise location and momentum of every atom in the universe then past and future values for any given time can be calculated from the laws of classical mechanics'.

1812 Grimms' Fairy Tales is first published under the title Kinder und Hausmärchen (Children's and Household Tales).

te rec Māori

1813 *Pride and Prejudice* by Jane Austen is published.

1815 Giovanni Belzoni, formerly a strongman at fairs, removes the colossal bust of Ramesses II, the Young Memnon, from the Ramesseum at Thebes.

1815 A meteorite ejected 11 million years previously from Mars falls in Chassigny, Haute-Marne, France.

1812 Lord Byron publicly defends the Luddites, a group of English textile artisans who violently protest against their replacement with unskilled workers and machinery.

1815 The metronome is invented by Johann Maelzel.

1815 Humphry Davy invents the Davy lamp allowing miners to work safely in the presence of flammable gases.

1815 Napoleon is exiled on the island of St Helena after defeat at the Battle of Waterloo.

1816 The stethoscope is invented by René Laennec.

1818 *Frankenstein; or, The Modern Prometheus* by Mary Shelley is published.

1818 *Ozymandias* by Percy Bysshe Shelley is published.

1819 The Prado museum in Madrid is completed.

1820 Antarctica is sighted for the first time by Imperial Russian Navy captain Fabian Gottlieb von Bellingshausen during his circumnavigation of the globe.

1820 Hans Christian Ørsted discovers the relationship between electricity and magnetism.

1820 The *Venus de Milo* statue is discovered on the Greek island of Milos.

1820 The Cato Street Conspiracy, a plot to murder all British cabinet ministers, is discovered.

1820 Spain sells part of Florida to the US for $5,000,000.

1821 Η σιδηροδρομική γραμμή Santa Fe εγκαθίσταται και γίνεται η πρώτη διεθνής διαδρομή του εμπορίου μεταξύ των Ηνωμένων Πολιτειών και του Μεξικού. Οι Αμερικάνοι πραγματοποιούσαν εμπορικές συναλλαγές με Ινδιάνες φυλές κατά μήκος της διαδρομής. 1821 Ο Μάικλ Φαραντέι κατασκεύασε τον μετασχηματιστή και τον ηλεκτρικό μηχανισμό μέσα από τον ηλεκτρομαγνητισμό, ανοίγοντας το δρόμο για την ανάπτυξη του βασικού 1821 Ο πρώτος σιδηρόδρομος σχεδιάζεται από τον Γάλλο βασιλιά Λουδοβίκο XVIII. 1822 Τα ιερογλυφικά της στήλης της παρακολουθεί επιπεδομετρία αλλά ήθελε να ξέρει ποσό αφαιρέθηκε από αρχαίο χρόνος. 1822 Ροζέτα αποκρυπτογραφούνται σύμφωνα με μ νόμιμα την πλευρά της γραφής και τα αρχαία ελληνικά. 1823 Απενέμοντα στον Τσαολς Μπάμπατζ 1.700 αιγυπτιακά ιερογλυφικά, την δημοτική γραφή και τα αρχαία ελληνικά. 1823 Απενέμοντα στον Τσαολς Μπάμπατζ 1.700 λίρες Αγγλίας για την ανάπτυξη του μηχανισμού διαφορισμού που εμποδίζεται μαστίγωμα διεξάγεται στο πριν 33.000 χρόνια με κόκκινο ώχρα, ανακαλύπτεται σε ασβεστολιθικά σπήλαια στη Νότια Ουαλία. 1823 Ο εντεκάχρονος τότε Φραντς Λιστ δίνει συναυλία οπού μετά την λήξη της λαμβάνει συγχαρητήρια από τον Λούντβιχ φον Μπετόβεν. 1823 Η μεξικανική αυτοκρατορία διαλύεται η Κόστα Ρίκα ενώνεται με τα κράτη του Ελ Σαλβαδόρ, της Γουατεμάλας, της Ονδούρας και της Νικαράγουας, και ονομάζονται Ηνωμένες Επαρχίες της Κεντρικής Αμερικής. 1823 Το παράδοξο του Όλμπερς περιγράφεται για πρώτη φορά. Το επίσης χαρακτηριζόμενο ως παράδοξο του νυχτερινού ουρανού', εξηγεί ότι ο νυχτερινός ουρανός είναι σκοτεινός αντικρούοντας την υπόθεση του άπειρου και αιώνια στατικού σύμπαντος. 1824 Ο Τζόν Ντίκενς (πατέρας του Καρόλου Ντίκενς) φυλακίζεται στη φυλακή Οφειλετών 'Marshalsea' για οφειλές σε αστοποιείο ύψους 40 λιρών και 10 σελινίων.

1821 THE SANTA FE TRAIL IS ESTABLISHED AND BECOMES THE FIRST INTERNATIONAL TRADE ROUTE BETWEEN THE UNITED STATES AND MEXICO. AMERICANS ROUTINELY TRADE WITH THE COMANCHE ALONG THE TRAIL. 1821 MICHAEL FARADAY DEMONSTRATES THE CONVERSION OF ELECTRICAL ENERGY INTO MECHANICAL ENERGY BY MEANS OF ELECTROMAGNETISM, PAVING THE WAY FOR THE DEVELOPMENT OF THE ELECTRIC MOTOR. 1821 THE FIRST COMMERCIALLY SUCCESSFUL CHRONOGRAPH IS INVENTED FOR KING LOUIS XVIII WHO ENJOYED WATCHING HORSE RACES, BUT WANTED TO KNOW EXACTLY HOW LONG EACH RACE LASTED. 1822 THE HIEROGLYPHS ON THE ROSETTA STONE ARE DECIPHERED USING THE FACT THAT THE INFORMATION APPEARS IN THREE SCRIPTS: ANCIENT EGYPTIAN HIEROGLYPHS, DEMOTIC SCRIPT AND ANCIENT GREEK. 1822 THE LAST PUBLIC WHIPPING IS CARRIED OUT IN EDINBURGH. 1822 A GROUP OF FREED SLAVES FROM THE UNITED STATES ARRIVE IN WEST AFRICA AND FOUND MONROVIA (LIBERIA). 1823 CHARLES BABBAGE IS AWARDED £1700 TO DEVELOP HIS DESIGN FOR THE DIFFERENCE ENGINE. 1823 THE RED LADY OF PAVILAND, AN UPPER PALEOLITHIC-ERA HUMAN MALE SKELETON 33,000 YEARS OLD DYED IN RED OCHRE, IS FOUND IN LIMESTONE CAVES IN SOUTH WALES. 1823 ELEVEN-YEAR-OLD FRANZ LISZT GIVES A CONCERT AFTER WHICH HE IS CONGRATULATED BY LUDWIG VAN BEETHOVEN. 1823 THE MEXICAN EMPIRE DISSOLVES; COSTA RICA JOINS EL SALVADOR, GUATEMALA, HONDURAS AND NICARAGUA AS THE UNITED PROVINCES OF CENTRAL AMERICA. 1823 OLBERS' PARADOX IS FIRST DESCRIBED. ALSO CALLED THE DARK NIGHT SKY PARADOX, IT EXPLAINS THAT THE DARKNESS OF THE NIGHT SKY CONFLICTS WITH THE ASSUMPTION OF AN INFINITE AND ETERNAL STATIC UNIVERSE. 1824 JOHN DICKENS (FATHER OF CHARLES DICKENS) IS IMPRISONED IN MARSHALSEA DEBTORS' PRISON FOR A DEBT OF £40 AND 10 SHILLINGS THAT HE OWES A BAKER.

1835 Charles Darwin reaches the Galapagos archipelago aboard the *HMS Beagle*.

1831 The *Hunchback* by Victor Hugo is p

1831 Robert Brown identifies the cell nucleus.

1831 Katsushika Hokusai creates the woodblock print series *Thirty-six Views of Mount Fuji*.

1830 *The Book of Mormon* by Joseph Smith is published.

1833 The first semi-conductor effect is recorded by Michael Faraday.

1834 The Spanish Inquisition, which began in the 15th century, is suppressed by royal decree.

Z

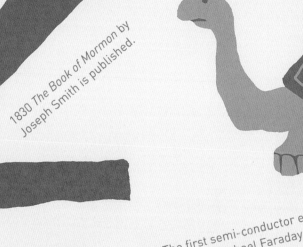

re-Dame
d.

1833 Alexandr Pushkin writes the poem
The Bronze Horseman: A Petersburg Tale.

1834 Eugène Delacroix paints
The Women of Algiers.

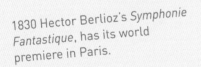

1830 Hector Berlioz's *Symphonie
Fantastique*, has its world
premiere in Paris.

1831 The Royal Zoological Society of
Dublin is founded by members of the
medical profession who wish to study
both living and dead animals.

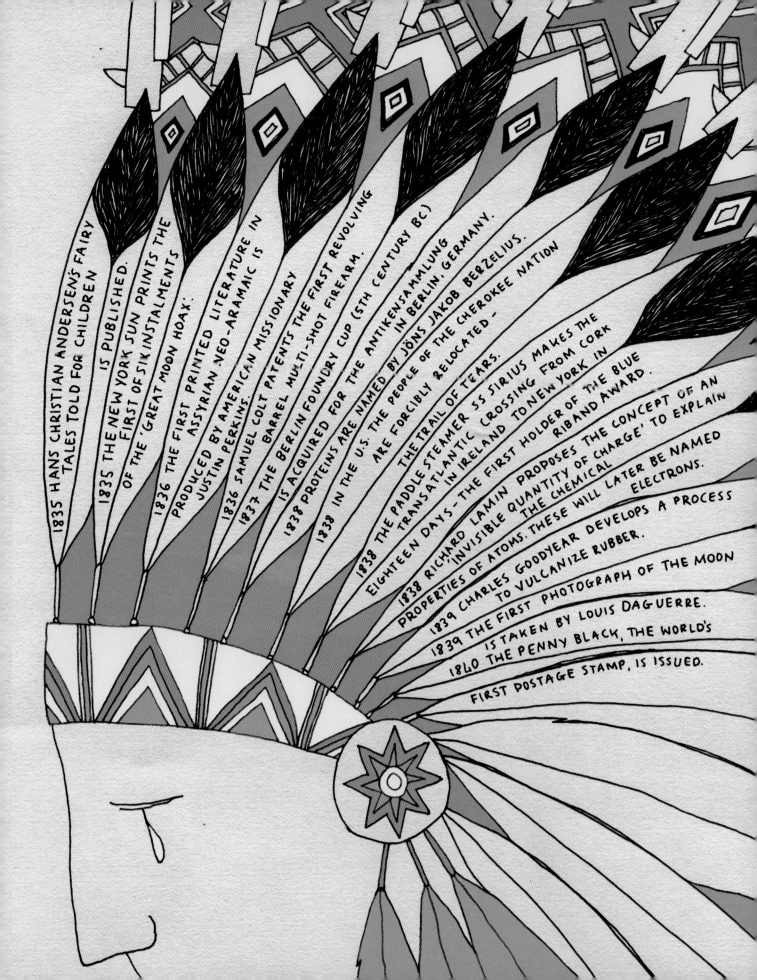

i^2 — j^2 — k^2

1841 Charles Mackay publishes
Extraordinary Popular Delusions and the Madness of Crowds.
1841 China cedes Hong Kong to Great Britain.
1843 William Rowan Hamilton writes the fundamental formula for quaternions
on Broome Bridge in Dublin, Ireland $i^2 = j^2 = k^2 = ijk = -1$.
1843 Joule studies the nature of heat, leading to the
theory of the conservation of energy.

1840 Samuel Morse is granted a patent for his invention of the telegraph.
1840 The Māori sign the Treaty of Waitangi, giving control to the British in exchange for protection and guaranteed Māori possession of their lands.
841 John Rand patents the first collapsible metal tube for artist's oil paint replacing breakable glass vials and leaky animal bladders.
Renoir later observes 'without paint in tubes, there would be no impressionism.'

ijk

-1

1844 The Great Auk becomes extinct.
1845 William Parsons, 3rd Earl of Rosse, builds the Leviathan of Parsonstown, a 72-inch reflecting telescope at Birr Castle in Ireland. It remains the world's largest telescope until the early 20th century.

1845 Frederick Douglass publishes his autobiography *Narrative of the Life of Frederick Douglass, an American Slave*.

1845 The first law relating to rugby boots is formulated: no player may wear projecting nails or iron plates on the heels or soles of his shoes or boots.

1846 The Oregon Treaty establishes the 49th parallel from the Rocky Mountains to the Strait of Juan de Fuca as the border between the United States and Canada.

1846 The anaesthetic properties of chloroform are discovered and used on an obstetric patient for the first time.

1848 Dante Gabriel Rossetti founds the Pre-Raphaelite Brotherhood with William Holman Hunt and John Everett Millais.

1846 Emily Brontë publishes *Wuthering Heights* under the pen name of Ellis Bell. The following year *Jane Eyre* by Charlotte Brontë is published under the pen name of Currer Bell.

1848 Kelvin establishes an absolute scale of temperature.

1848 The campaign for women's suffrage in the US begins at the Seneca Falls Convention. The following year Elizabeth Blackwell becomes the world's first openly identified woman to graduate from a medical school.

1848 The California Gold Rush is prompted when James Marshall finds flakes of gold at Sutter's Mill, in Coloma.

1849 Fyodor Dostoyevsky serves four years of exile with hard labour at a Katorga prison camp in Omsk, Siberia.

1849 Fizeau's rotating wheel becomes the first terrestrial method used for measuring the velocity of light.

1846 The Great Famine begins in Ireland when three quarters of the potato crop is lost to blight *Phytophthora Infestans*.

BASIC PRINCIPLES OF THE SECOND LAW OF THERMODYNAMICS.

1850 THE TARA BROOCH (700 AD) IS FOUND IN COUNTY MEATH, IRELAND.

ON A 67M LONG WIRE, IS SUSPENDED FROM THE DOME OF THE PANTHÉON IN PARIS.

MODERN CHESS TOURNAMENT IS WON BY ADOLF ANDERSSEN.

1851 MOBY-DICK BY HERMAN MELVILLE IS PUBLISHED.

ASSEMBLY.

1854 FLORENCE NIGHTINGALE LEAVES FOR THE CRIMEA WITH 38 OTHER NURSES.

1850 RUDOLF CLAUSIUS PROPOSES THE

1851 FOUCAULT'S PENDULUM, A 28KG BRASS-COATED LEAD BOB

1851 JOHN EVERETT MILLAIS PAINTS OPHELIA.

1851 THE GREAT EXHIBITION IS HELD AT THE CRYSTAL PALACE IN LONDON.

1851 THE FIRST

1851 VICTOR HUGO USES THE PHRASE 'UNITED STATES OF EUROPE' IN A SPEECH TO THE FRENCH NATIONAL

1854 GEORGE BOOLE DEVELOPS BOOLEAN ALGEBRA BASED ON THE MATHEMATICAL ANALYSIS OF LOGIC.

1855 SAFETY MATCHES USING RED PHOSPHORUS ON THE STRIKING SURFACE ARE INTRODUCED.

NORTH
AMERICA

Newfoundland

On the Origin
of Species

N
NW NE
W E
SW SE
S

1855

1855   Alexander II, later known as Alexander
        the Liberator for freeing the serfs, becomes
        Emperor of Russia. His reign ends in
        1881 when he is killed in a fourth
        assassination attempt.
1855   David Livingstone discovers and names
        Victoria Falls - also known as Mosi-oa-Tunya
        (the smoke that thunders) - on the
        Zambezi river.
1856   Gustave Flaubert's *Madame Bovary* is
        published. Flaubert is accused of obscenity
        by public prosecutors and put on trial the
        following year.
1858   Felix Mendelssohn's *Wedding March* is played
        at the marriage of Queen Victoria's daughter
        Victoria to Crown Prince Frederick of Prussia.
1858   *Gray's Anatomy* is published.

1860

Ireland

Great
Britian

Gray's
Anatomy

Big Ben

Möbius strip

EUROPE

AFRICA

1858   Möbius and Listing introduce the Möbius strip.
1858   The first transatlantic telegraph cable is
         laid across the floor of the Atlantic from
         Valentia Island in Ireland to Heart's Content
         in eastern Newfoundland. The communication
         time between North America and Europe is
         reduced from ten days to minutes.
1859   Big Ben is completed.
1859   Building begins on the Suez Canal in Egypt.
1859   *On the Origin of Species* by Charles Darwin
         µis published.
1859   *The Rubáiyát of Omar Khayyám* is published -
         Edward FitzGerald's translation of a selection
         of poems written by the 12th century Persian
         poet, mathematician and astronomer.
1860   Bunsen and Kirchhoff develop analytical
         spectroscopy.

1863 The Gettysburg Address by President Abraham Lincoln.

1864 Frederic William Burton paints Hellelil and Hildebrand known in English as Meeting on the Turret Stairs.

1865 Rudolf Clausius introduces the concept of entropy.

1862 Louis Pasteur develops a process in which liquids such as milk are heated to kill most bacteria and moulds already present within them - Later known as pasteurization.

1860 Florence Nightingale opens the first non-religious nursing school in the world.

1861 Auguste the excavation of Edfu from the west bank

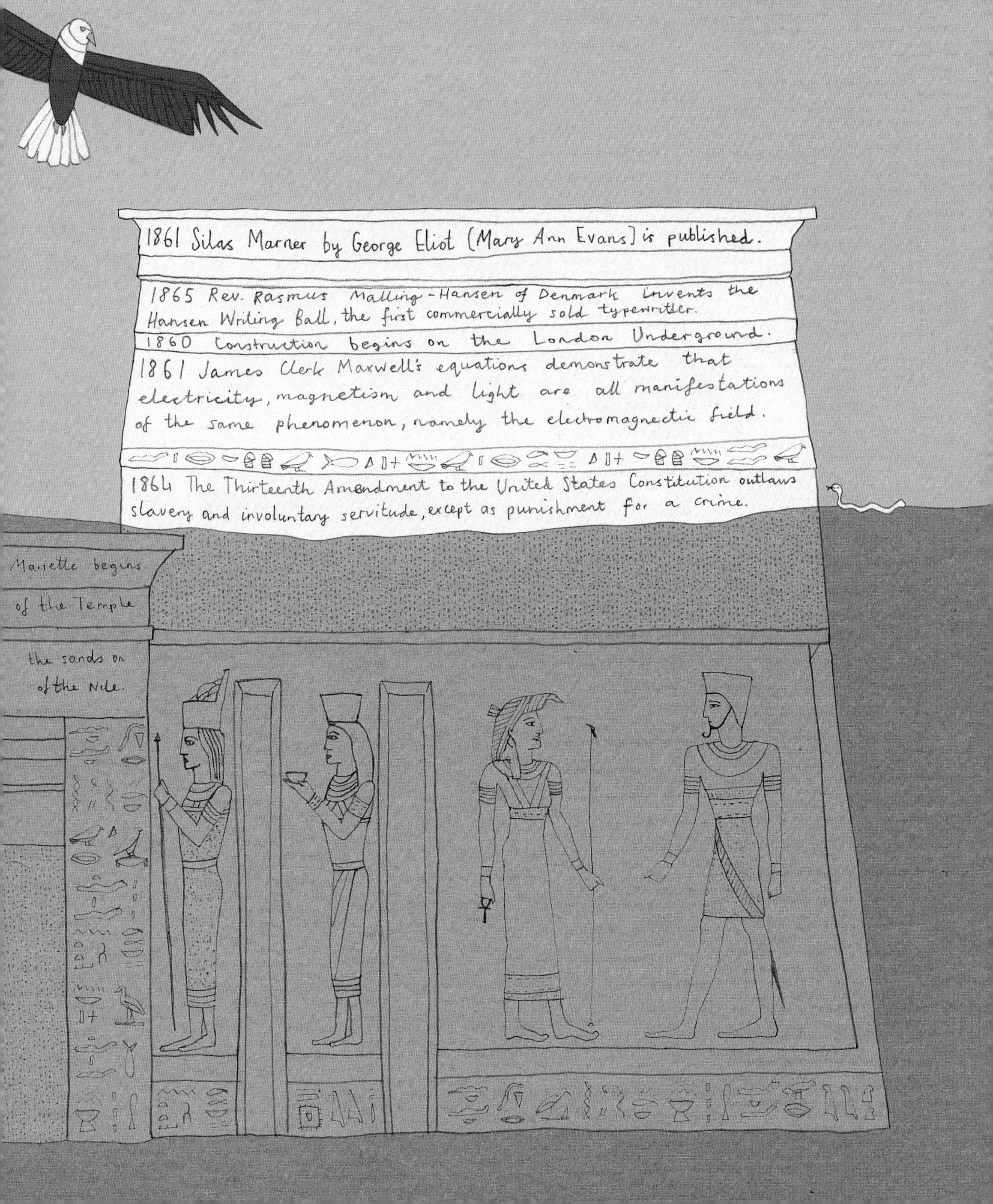

1861 Silas Marner by George Eliot (Mary Ann Evans) is published.

1865 Rev. Rasmus Malling-Hansen of Denmark invents the Hansen Writing Ball, the first commercially sold typewriter.

1860 Construction begins on the London Underground.

1861 James Clerk Maxwell's equations demonstrate that electricity, magnetism and light are all manifestations of the same phenomenon, namely the electromagnetic field.

1864 The Thirteenth Amendment to the United States Constitution outlaws slavery and involuntary servitude, except as punishment for a crime.

Mariette begins

of the Temple

the sands on

of the Nile.

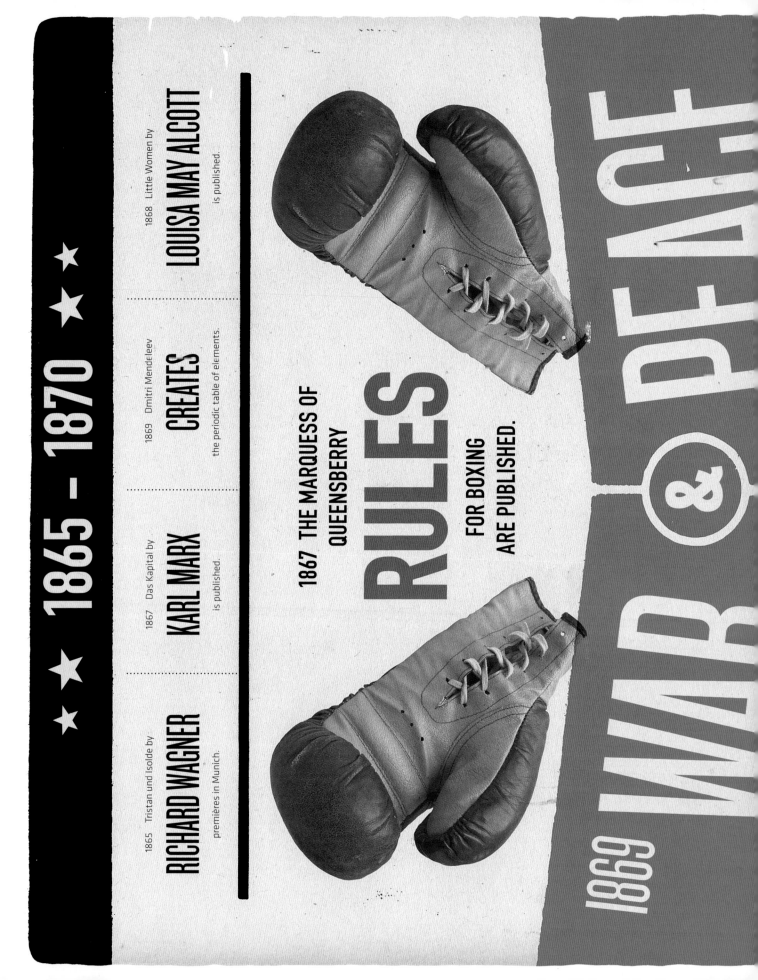

★ ★ **1865 – 1870** ★ ★

1865 Tristan und Isolde by
RICHARD WAGNER
premières in Munich.

1867 Das Kapital by
KARL MARX
is published.

1867 THE MARQUESS OF
QUEENSBERRY
RULES
FOR BOXING
ARE PUBLISHED.

1869 Dmitri Mendeleev
CREATES
the periodic table of elements.

1868 Little Women by
LOUISA MAY ALCOTT
is published.

1869 **WAR & PEACE**

1870

ROBERT KOCH

LOUIS PASTEUR &

PASTEUR & KOCH

establish the germ theory of disease.

by LEO TOLSTOY is published

1868 DANTE GABRIEL ROSSETTI paints a portrait of **JANE MORRIS**, the wife of **WILLIAM MORRIS**, titled

THE BLUE SILK DRESS

1865 GREGOR MENDEL founds the new science of genetics, based on his cultivation and testing of some

29,000 PEA PLANTS

1867 Colonies now known as **NOVA SCOTIA**, **NEW BRUNSWICK**, **ONTARIO** and **QUEBEC** join to create the

DOMINION OF CANADA

1867 THE UNITED STATES accepts the Russian Emperor Alexander II's offer to sell Alaska for $7.2 million.

1869 THE SUEZ CANAL opens, connecting the Mediterranean with the Red Sea.

1869 JOHN TYNDALL demonstrates and explains the Tyndall effect – why the sky is blue and the sunset is red.

1869 Édouard Manet creates the series of paintings titled

THE EXECUTION OF EMPEROR MAXIMILIAN

depicting the execution by firing squad of Emperor Maximilian I of the short-lived Second Mexican Empire.

1875 The first
organized indoor game
of ice hockey is played at the Victoria
Skating Rink in Montreal, Canada.

1875
The Metre Convention
is signed in Paris.

1871 The first
rugby union international
game results in a 4–1 win by
Scotland over England.

1871 Publication
of *The Descent of Man
and Selection in Relation to
Sex* by Charles Darwin includes his first
formal use of the term evolution.

1874
The Agra
canal opens in India.

1871 *Aida* by
Giuseppe Verdi
is first performed at the
Khedivial Opera House in Cairo.

1873 *Anna Karenina* by Leo Tolstoy is published in serial instalments in the periodical *The Russian Messenger*.

1874 The New York Zoo hoax - a New York Herald article warns that dangerous animals from Central Park Zoo are loose in the city causing widespread panic despite the article ending with the words 'the entire story given above is a pure fabrication.'

1872 Claude Monet paints *Impression, Sunrise*.

1874 Edvard Grieg starts composing the incidental music for Ibsen's play *Peer Gynt*.

1872 Yellowstone National Park is established as the first National Park in the world.

1872 The science of oceanography is born when the HMS Challenger expedition departs from Portsmouth with five scientists and one artist aboard – they will discover 4,700 previously unknown species.

1873 Charles Hermite proves that the mathematical constant e is a transcendental number.

1875 The Bombay Stock Exchange in India is establi

1875 A pre Columbian Chac Mool sculpture is exca

Chichen Itza, Yucatán. It will later influence Henry M

partial bankruptcy and places its finances in the

opens in Berlin. It produces legal tender (the Gol

gold is abandoned.   1876 Alexander Graham b

successful call saying.   "Mr Watson, come

paints Dancers practising   at the Barre. 1877 Au

match. The series becomes known as The Ashes. 187;

Bolshoi Theatre in Moscow. 1878 Sallie Gardner

24 photographs in a fast-motion series that are sho

publishes 'Human, All Too Human: A Book for Free

Madison Square Garden by William Henry Vanderbi

by Henrik Ibsen is published and premières in Copenl

to write an alternative ending in keeping with tradit;

d becoming the first stockbrokers' association in Asia.
ted from the Platform of the Eagles and Jaguars at
re's sculpture style. 1875 The Ottoman state declares
rds of its European creditors. 1876 The Reichsbank
ark) until 1914 when the link between the mark and
inverts the Telephone and ‎ makes the first
re, I want to see you." ‎ 1877 Edgar Degas
alia beats England in the ‎ first cricket Test
Tchaikovsky's ballet 'Swan Lake' premieres at the
a Gallop, the first motion picture, is recorded using
on a zoopraxiscope. 1878 Friedrich Nietzsche
pirits.' 1879 New York City's Gilmore's Garden is renamed
, and is opened to the public. 1879 'A Doll's House'
ger. For the play's German debut, Ibsen is forced
al expectations as to how a wife and mother would act.

1880   Greenwich Mean Time is legally
        adopted in Britain.

1881   The world's oldest international sport
        federation, *Federation Internationale
        de Gymnastique*, is founded.

1882   Ferdinand von Lindeman proves
        that π is transcendental.

1882   Heinrich Koch isolates Tuberculosis
        bacillus.

1883   *The Adventures of Pinocchio* by Carlo
        Collodi is published.

1883   The quagga – half zebra, half horse
        – once very common in South Africa,
        becomes extinct.

1884   Anton Chekhov qualifies as a
        physician although he makes little
        money from the profession and treats
        the poor for free.

1884   The Hungarian Royal Opera House
        in Budapest opens to the public.

1884   Georges Seurat begins to paint *A
        Sunday Afternoon on the Island of La
        Grande Jatte*, the first painting in
        the pointillist style initiating Neo-
        impressionism.

1885   Nicola Tesla redesigns Edison's
        inefficient motor and generators
        based on a promise (he claims Edison
        made) of $50,000. Tesla inquires
        about payment and Edison replies,
        'Tesla, you don't understand our
        American humor' and offers him an
        increase in salary from $18 a week to
        $28. Tesla immediately resigns.

1885   Carl Fabergé makes his first jewelled
        egg for Tsar Alexander III of Russia.

c1885   Berthe Morisot paints *Girl on a Divan*.

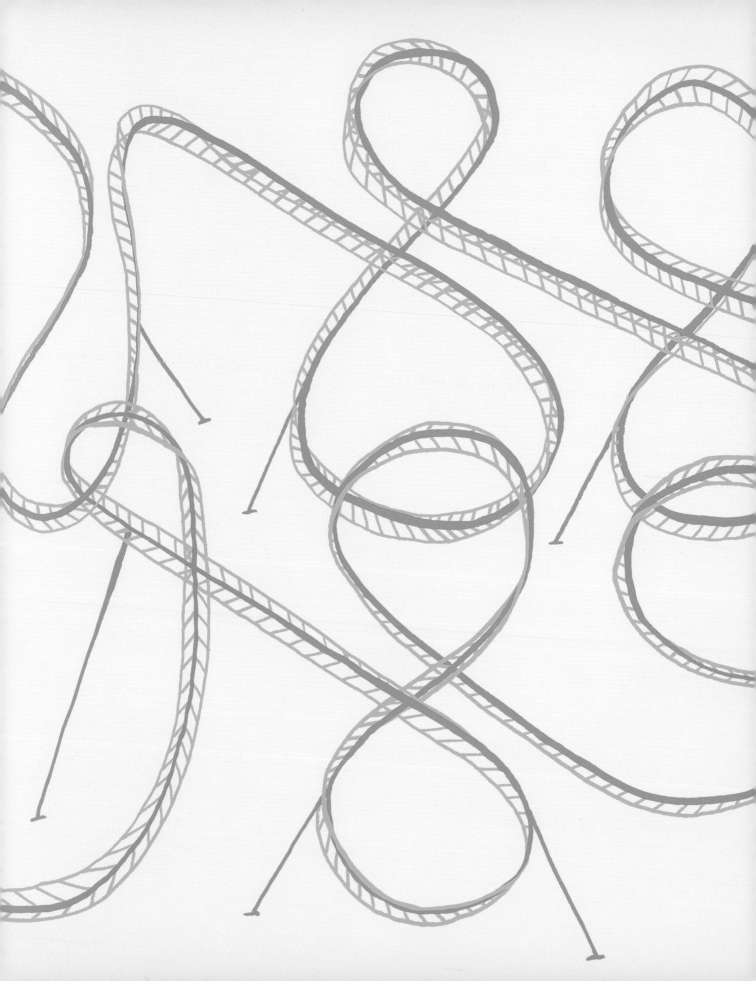

1885 The rollercoaster is patented.

1886 The first official world Chess Championship is held with Wilhelm Steinitz beating the Polish-born master Johannes Zukertort.

1886 The world's first motor car, the Benz Patent Motorwagen, is unveiled by Karl Benz.

1887 The Michelson and Morley experiments refute the ether theory.

1887 The first All-Ireland Football and Hurling Championships are played.

1888 Hertz demonstrates radio waves, a part of the electromagnetic spectrum.

1888 Stanislavski takes the role of the Knight in a production of Alexander Pushkin's *The Miserly Knight*.

1888 Thomas Edison holds a press conference to demonstrate his gramophone, playing one of the first recordings of music ever made.

1888 Vincent van Gogh paints *The Sunflowers*. He associated yellow with hope and friendship saying it was 'an idea expressing gratitude'. He hangs the painting in the guest bedroom in Arles in anticipation of the arrival of his friend Gauguin.

1889 The Eiffel Tower is completed. Seventy-two names of French scientists, engineers and notables are engraved on the structure but no women are included in the list.

1890 Tsar Alexander III of Russia establishes the Trans-Siberian Railway.

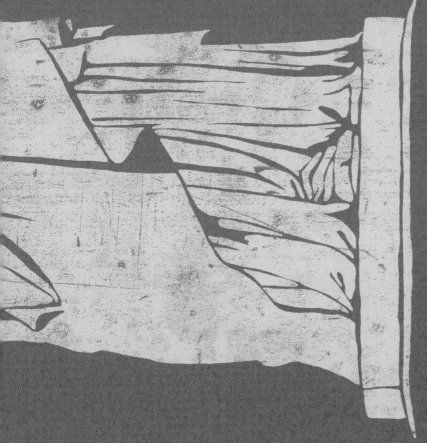

1890 The first known crossword puzzle appears in the Italian magazine *Il Secolo Illustrato*. **1891** Basketball is invented by James Naismith in the USA. **1891** Oscar Wilde's *The Soul of Man under Socialism* is published. **1892** The Ellis Island immigrant station officially opens on 1st January. A 14 year-old Irish girl, Annie Moore, is the first passenger to register. **1893** New Zealand becomes the first country to give women the right to vote in national elections. **1893** At the Chicago World Fair, Nikola Tesla lights a wireless gas-discharge lamp using a high-voltage high-frequency alternating current. **1893** Maria Montessori enters the medical program at the University of Rome. Her attendance at classes with men in the presence of a naked body is deemed inappropriate and she is required to perform her dissections of cadavers alone, after hours. **1894** Anton Chekhov begins writing *The Seagull* in a lodge in the orchard of his small estate in Melikhovo, a town 40 miles south of Moscow. **1894** Alexandre Yersin isolates the bacterium that caused the third pandemic of the bubonic plague. **1894** Ireland wins the Rugby Triple Crown for the first time. **1894** *The Time Machine* by H G Wells is published. **1895** The first Venice Biennale is held.

1895   The London School of
        Economics is co-founded
        by George Bernard Shaw.

1895   Wilhelm Röntgen
        discovers X-rays.

1895   Ivan Pavlov analyzes the
        saliva and response of dogs
        to food under different
        conditions.

1895   *The Importance of Being
        Earnest, A Trivial Comedy
        for Serious People* by Oscar
        Wilde is first performed at
        the St James's Theatre
        in London.

1896   The first modern Olympic
        games are held in Athens.

1897   *Dracula* by Bram Stoker
        is published.

1897   Aspirin (acetylsalicylic
        acid) is first isolated by
        Felix Hoffmann in Germany.

1897   Guglielmo Marconi
        sends the first wireless
        communication over
        open sea.

1898   Joshua Slocum completes
        the first single-handed
        circumnavigation of the
        world in *The Spray* (11.2m).

1898   Radium is discovered by
        Marie Skłodowska-Curie
        and her husband Pierre in
        a uraninite sample. Ernest
        Rutherford identifies alpha
        and beta particles.

1900   *The Wonderful Wizard of
        Oz* by L Frank Baum is
        published.

c1900   Paul Cézanne paints
        The Bathers.

1900 KARL LANDSTEINER IDENTIFIES THE MAIN BLOOD GROUPS.

1900 MAX PLANCK POSTULATES THAT ELECTROMAGNETIC ENERGY CAN ONLY BE EMITTED IN QUANTIZED FORM – THE BIRTH OF QUANTUM PHYSICS.

1900 THE ANTIKYTHERA MECHANISM, AN ANCIENT DEVICE USED TO CALCULATE ASTRONOMICAL POSITIONS, IS RECOVERED FROM A WRECK IN THE AEGEAN SEA.

1901 A SEMI-CONDUCTOR CRYSTAL RECTIFIER FOR DETECTING RADIO WAVES, DESCRIBED AS *CAT'S WHISKERS*, IS PATENTED BY CHANDRA BOSE.

1902 FLIRTING IN PUBLIC IS OUTLAWED IN NEW YORK STATE.

1902 AUGUSTE RODIN SCULPTS *THE THINKER*.

1902 IRISH BORN MARY HARRIS, LATER KNOWN AS MOTHER JONES, IS CONSIDERED TO BE THE *'MOST DANGEROUS WOMAN IN AMERICA'* DUE TO HER MILITANCY WITH THE LABOUR UNIONS.

1902 GUSTAV KLIMT CREATES *THE BEETHOVEN FRIEZE* FOR THE VIENNESE *SECESSION* BUILDING.

1903 THE FIRST TOUR DE FRANCE IS HELD TO INCREASE PAPER SALES FOR THE MAGAZINE *L'AUTO* (L'ÉQUIPE).

1903 THE WRIGHT BROTHERS BUILD AND FLY THE FIRST SUCCESSFUL AEROPLANE AT KITTYHAWK, NORTH CAROLINA.

1903 EDWIN S. PORTER'S FILM *THE GREAT TRAIN ROBBERY* STARRING BRONCHO BILLY ANDERSON, IS RELEASED.

1904 JAMES JOYCE HAS HIS FIRST OUTING WITH NORA BARNACLE IN DUBLIN ON JUNE 16TH, THE DATE ON WHICH HIS NOVEL *ULYSSES* IS BASED, NOW CELEBRATED AS *BLOOMSDAY*.

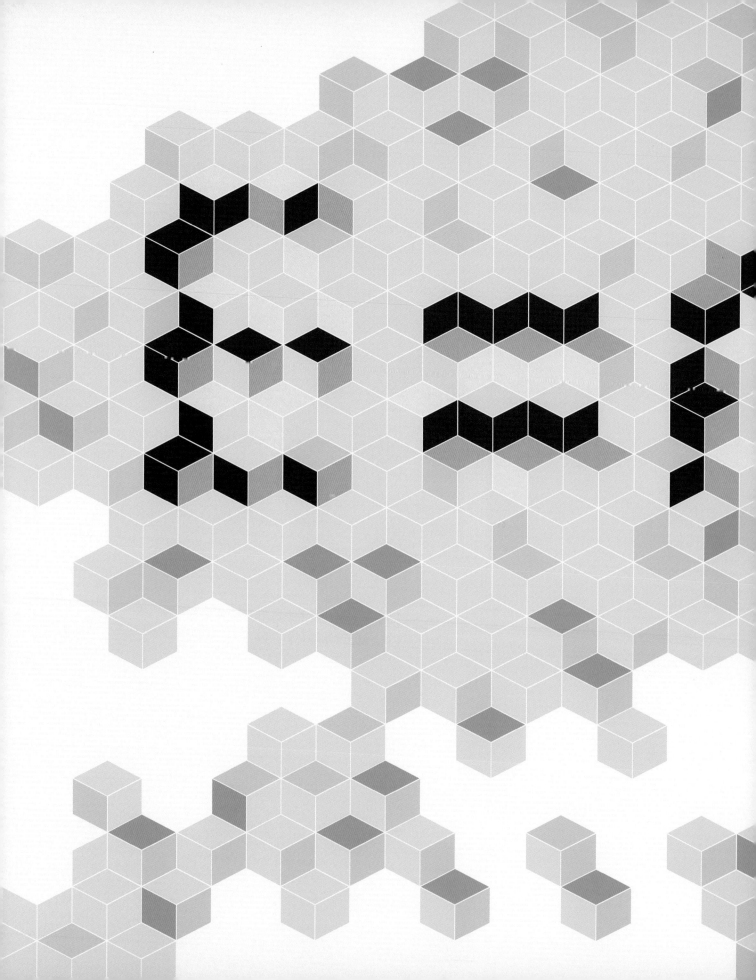

1905 'Sensible and responsible women do not want to vote' states Grover Cleveland, U.S. President.

1905 Albert Einstein proposes the law of the photoelectric effect and special relativity $E=mc^2$ – his 'Miraculous Year'.

1905 Sigmund Freud's *Three Essays on the Theory of Sexuality and Jokes and their Relation to the Unconscious* is published.

1905 A dimple pattern is applied to golf balls maximising lift and minimising drag.

1905 Tsar Nicholas II agrees to a constitution, devolution of some power to the Duma, and a free press.

1907 The Suffragettes march through London, led by Emily Pankhurst.

1907 George Soper identifies Mary Mallon as an asymptomatic carrier of typhoid in New York – Typhoid Mary.

1907 The first *Casa dei Bambini* (Children's House) overseen by Maria Montessori opens in Rome.

1908 Kristian Birkeland proposes that the Aurora borealis phenomenon is connected to geomagnetic field lines.

1909 Lansteiner, Levaditi and Popper discover the polio virus.

1909 Pablo Picasso and Georges Braque invent *Analytic Cubism*.

1910 The Casa Milà is constructed in Barcelona.

1911   *Alexander's Ragtime Band* by Irving Berlin becomes a major hit.

1911   Roald Amundsen and his team reach the South Pole.

1912   Photo finish is used for the first time at the Summer Olympics in Stockholm.

1912   A German archaeological team discovers the Nefertiti bust in Thutmose's workshop in Amarna, Egypt.

of Vladimir Lenin decides to make *Pravda* its official mouthpiece.

1912   RMS *Titanic* departs on her maiden voyage from Cork, Ireland.

1913   The premiere of Stravinsky's *Rite of Spring* is presented as a ballet, choreographed by Vaslav Nijinsky, in Paris. The avant-garde nature of the music and choreography causes a near-riot in the audience.

1913   Marcel Proust pays for publication of the first volume of *À la Recherche du Temps Perdu.*

1913   Neils Bohr proposes the quantum theory of atomic orbits.

1913   Henry Ford installs the first modern assembly line for wwwmotor cars.

1914   On Christmas Eve during World War 1, British and German soldiers climb out from the trenches into 'no man's land' and sing carols while sharing cake and cigars. A spontaneous truce extends for hundreds of miles amongst thousands of soldiers.

1914   The Panama Canal opens.

1915   Ernest Shackelton and his trans-Antarctic Expedition team spend the polar winter on their ship *Endurance* as it is slowly crushed by ice in the Weddell Sea, on the coast of Antarctica.

1916

DADAISM

c1920 Irish architect Eileen Grey designs the Bibendum Chair

1916

Giorgio de Chirico paints *The Disquieting Muses* inspiring Sylvia Plath's poem of the same title, written in 1957.

Margaret Sanger opens the first birth control clinic in the United States leading to her arrest for distributing information on contraception.

The Easter Rising in Ireland.
The Battle of the Somme in France.

Shackleton
and five crew members
depart from

1916

ElePhant Island

in a small open boat
on a rescue mission.
They reach the
uninhabited southern
coast of South Georgia
15 days later having survived an 800 nautical mile trip on the southern ocean.

an art movement of the
European avant-garde,
begins in Zurich,
Switzerland.

1915 Einstein's propoSes the General Theory of RelativitY.

1918 Countess Markievicz is the first woman to be elected to the British House of Commons. 1918 Reconstruction begins on the Prambanan, a 9th-century Hindu temple compound in Central Java. 1919 Desert Gold, a New Zealand thoroughbred racehorse, wins her 19th race in succession. 1919 Aurthur Eddington observes gravity bending starlight during a solar eclipse - the first supporting evidence for Einstein's General Relativity prediction. 1920 Mustafa Kemal Atatürk becomes president of Turkey.

c1920 coco chanel designs what will become known as the little black dress 1920 prohibition is enforced in the united states 1922 ulysses by james joyce is published by sylvia beach in paris 1922 frederick banting and charles best discover insulin 1922 the irish free state is formed 1922 the tomb of tutankhamun is discovered in egypt 1923 the 24 hours of le mans sports car race is held for the first time 1923 ernest hemmingway takes up bull fighting and big game hunting in spain 1924 louis de broglie proposes the theory that matter has a wave-like nature 1924 the first winter olympic games are held in chamonix france 1924 george gershwin composes rhapsody in blue 1925 john logie baird successfully transmits the first televised silhouette images in motion television

1925 herbe
develops tl
for univers
for the bau
letterhead

rt bayer
ne designs
al lettering
haus

1930 MAHATMA GANDHI LEADS A MARCH FROM AHMEDABAD TO THE COAST OF INDIA AND PICKS UP SALT IN DEFIANCE OF THE SALT TAX, TRIGGERING THE NON-VIOLENT CIVIL DISOBEDIENCE MOVEMENT IN INDIA.

1929 SHOSTAKOVICH COMPOSES THE FILM SCORE FOR THE SILENT MOVIE THE NEW BABYLON. SET DURING THE 1871 PARIS COMMUNE.

1927 MIES VAN DER ROHE DESIGNS THE GERMAN PAVILION FOR THE INTERNATIONAL EXPOSITION IN BARCELONA.

1927 THE FIRST WORLD SNOOKER CHAMPIONSHIP IS PLAYED IN BIRMINGHAM, ENGLAND.

1927 TO THE LIGHTHOUSE BY VIRGINIA WOOLF IS PUBLISHED.

THE EXCAVATION OF PETRA IN JORDAN.

THE WORLD'S FIRST LIQUID-FUELLED ROCKE

1929 THE GRAF ZEPPELIN BECOMES THE

ARD BUILDS AND LAUNCHES 1929

1925 THE GREAT GATSBY

1928 PAUL DIRAC PREDICTS THE EXISTENCE OF ANTIMATTER.

1928 ALEXANDER FLEMING DISCOVERS THE ANTIBIOTIC EFFECT OF PENICILLIN.

1927 THE JAZZ SINGER STARRING AL JOLSON IS THE FIRST FEATURE LENGTH 'TALKIE' FILM RELEASED.

1929 HERGE'S TINTIN FIRST APPEARS.

FIRST AIRSHIP TO CIRCUMNAVIGATE THE WORLD.

1926 ROBERT GOD

1928 BY F SCOTT FITZGERALD IS PUBLISHED.

1930-1935

1930 URUGUAY HOSTS, AND WINS, THE FIRST SOCCER WORLD CUP

1930 THE FIRST DIVE IN A BATHYSPHERE IS MADE BY OTIS BARTON AND CHARLES BEEBE. THEY DESCEND TO A DEPTH OF 183M.

1931 THE EMPIRE STATE BUILDING OPENS.

1931 HISTOIRE DE BABAR BY JEAN DE BRUNHOFF IS PUBLISHED.

1932 JOHN COCKCROFT AND ERNEST WALTON SPLIT THE ATOM USING A PARTICLE ACCELERATOR.

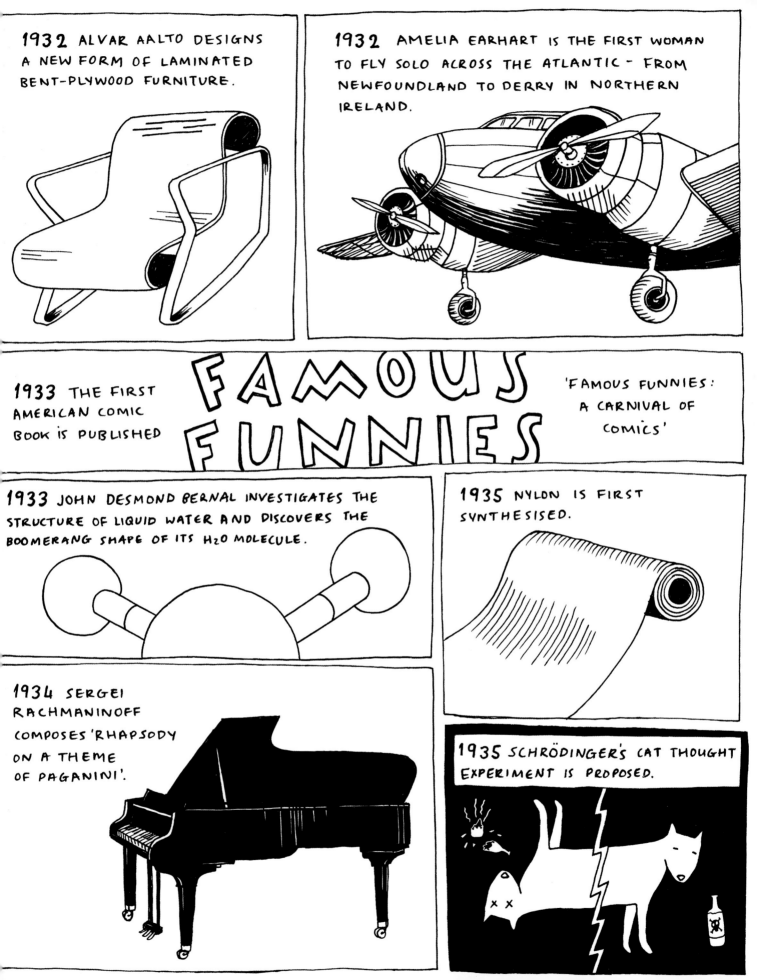

1932 ALVAR AALTO DESIGNS A NEW FORM OF LAMINATED BENT-PLYWOOD FURNITURE.

1932 AMELIA EARHART IS THE FIRST WOMAN TO FLY SOLO ACROSS THE ATLANTIC - FROM NEWFOUNDLAND TO DERRY IN NORTHERN IRELAND.

1933 THE FIRST AMERICAN COMIC BOOK IS PUBLISHED

FAMOUS FUNNIES

'FAMOUS FUNNIES: A CARNIVAL OF COMICS'

1933 JOHN DESMOND BERNAL INVESTIGATES THE STRUCTURE OF LIQUID WATER AND DISCOVERS THE BOOMERANG SHAPE OF ITS H_2O MOLECULE.

1935 NYLON IS FIRST SYNTHESISED.

1934 SERGEI RACHMANINOFF COMPOSES 'RHAPSODY ON A THEME OF PAGANINI'.

1935 SCHRÖDINGER'S CAT THOUGHT EXPERIMENT IS PROPOSED.

1935. The first paperback Penguin Books are published.

1936. Gymnastics for women is added to the Olympic program at the Berlin Games.

1939. Alan Turing's electromechanical machine (the Bombe) deciphers the Enigma codes.

1938 Freda Kahlo paints the first of her self-portraits with a monkey.

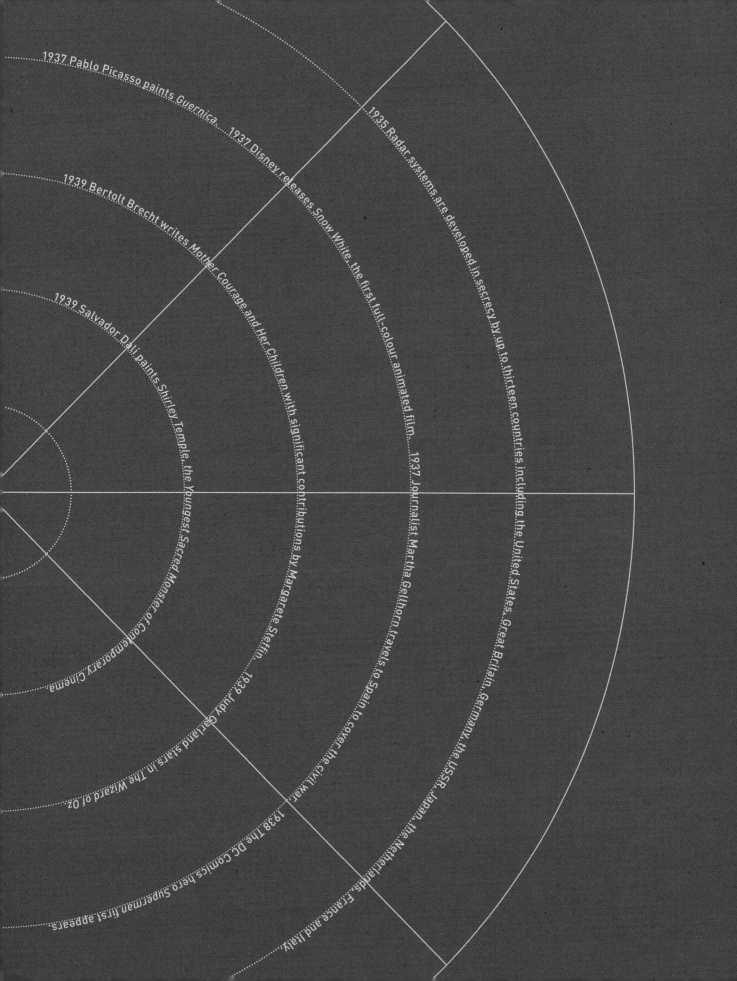

1937 Pablo Picasso paints Guernica.

1937 Disney releases Snow White, the first full-colour animated film.

1939 Bertolt Brecht writes Mother Courage and Her Children, with significant contributions by Margarete Steffin.

1939 Salvador Dalí paints Shirley Temple, the Youngest Sacred Monster of Contemporary Cinema.

1935 Radar systems are developed in secrecy by up to thirteen countries including the United States, Great Britain, Germany, the USSR, Japan, the Netherlands, France and Italy.

1937 Journalist Martha Gellhorn travels to Spain to cover the civil war.

1939 Judy Garland stars in The Wizard of Oz.

1938 The DC Comics hero Superman first appears.

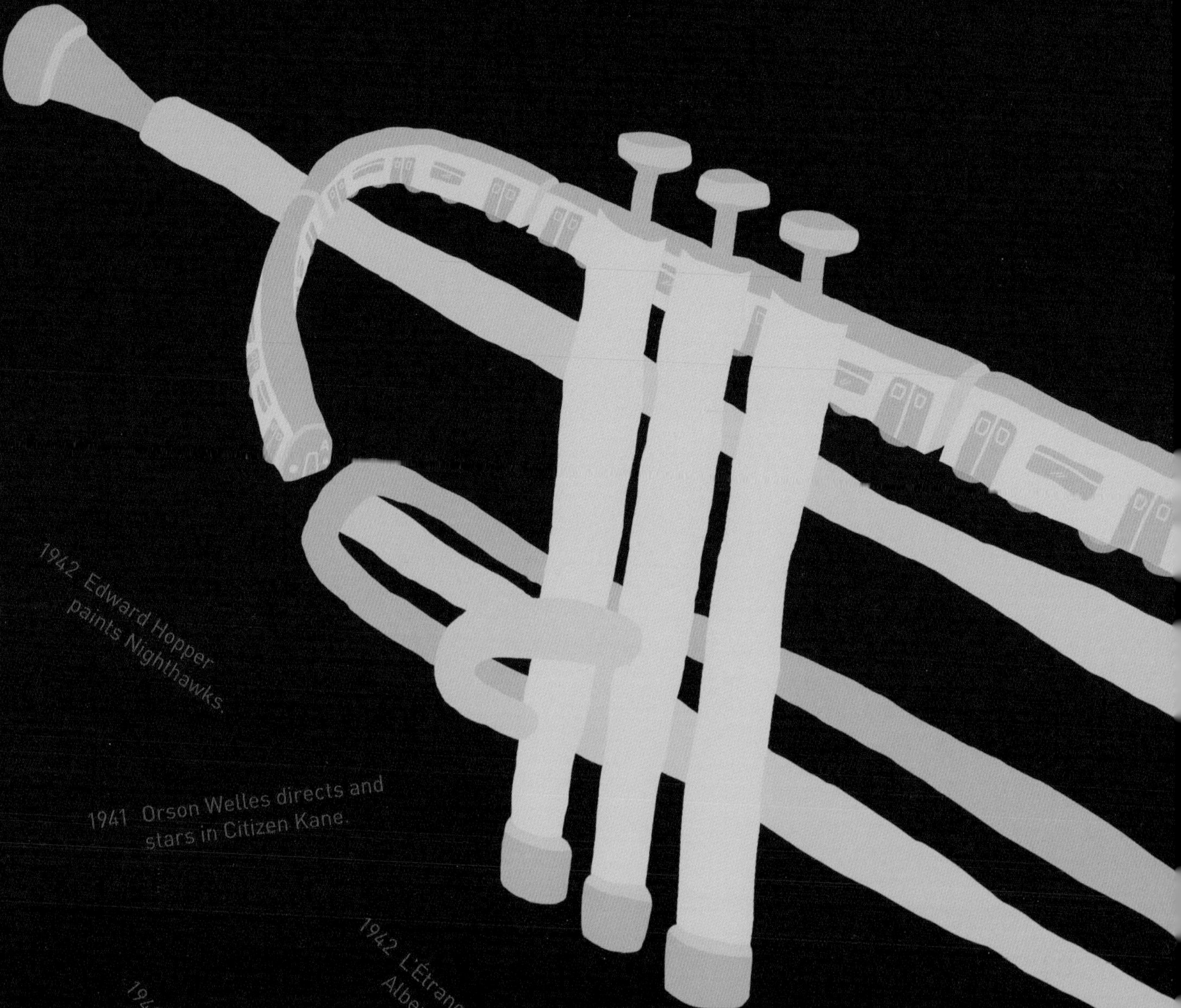

1942 Edward Hopper
paints Nighthawks.

1941 Orson Welles directs and
stars in Citizen Kane.

1942 L'Étranger (The Outsider) by
Albert Camus is published.

1940 The first metallic hip
replacement surgery is
performed at Johns Hopkins
Hospital, USA. Twenty
years later the use of ivory
prostheses is pioneered in
Mandalay, Burma.

1941 A special Monopoly edition
is created for World War II
prisoners of war. Hidden inside
are items such as maps and
compasses to aid escapes.

1940 Upper Paleolithic art 17,300
years old is discovered in
the Lascaux Cave in the
Dordogne, France.

1942 Enrico Fermi achieves the first self-sustaining fission chain reaction.

1944 The International Monetary Fund (IMF) and the World Bank are founded.

1941 Billy Strayhorn's Take the 'A' Train is recorded and becomes the signature tune of the Duke Ellington Orchestra. The title refers to the new subway running from eastern Brooklyn into Harlem.

1941 Dumbo is produced by Walt Disney.

1945 The 'Trinity' test, the first detonation of a nuclear weapon, takes place in the New Mexico desert on 16th July.

1945 The concentration camp at Auschwitz is liberated by Soviet troops on 27th January, now Holocaust Memorial Day.

1945-19

1946 SOVIET SCHOOL PRESENT A WOODEN REPLICA GREAT SEAL OF THE UNITED STAT TO THE US AMBASSADOR AT THE MOSCOW EMBASSY. IN 1952 IT IS DISCOVERED THAT THE SEAL CONTAINS A MICROPHONE.

1949 '1984' BY GEORGE ORWELL
IS PUBLISHED.

ISO

1949 THE FIRST ATOMIC CLOCK IS CONSTRUCTED.

1947 THE ANNEX: DIARY NOTES FROM 14 JUNE 1942 – 1 AUGUST 1944 IS PUBLISHED IN AMSTERDAM AND LATER TRANSLATED AS ANNE FRANK: THE DIARY OF A YOUNG GIRL.

1946 COLONEL JUAN PERÓN IS ELECTED PRESIDENT OF ARGENTINA AND HIS WIFE, EVA PERÓN (EVITA), IS PUT IN CHARGE OF LABOUR RELATIONS.

1950 I, ROBOT A COLLECTION OF NINE STORIES BY ISAAC ASIMOV IS PUBLISHED.

1949 THE CARBON-14 ISOTOPE IS FIRST USED FOR RADIOCARBON DATING OF ARCHAEOLOGICAL AND GEOLOGICAL SAMPLES.

1949 LE DEUXIÈME SEXE BY SIMONE DE BEAUVOIR IS PUBLISHED.

1946 PARKER BROTHERS BRINGS OUT GAME OF RICH UNCLE FEATURING RICH UNCLE PENNYBAGS.

1946 PIAGGIO DESIGNS THE VESPA SCOOTER.

CHILDREN OF THE

1947 INDIA BECOMES AN INDEPENDENT STATE UNDER PRIME MINISTER PANDIT NEHRU.

1950 Polio vaccines are developed independently by Koprowski, Salk and Sabin. In 1962 Sabin's live vaccine (Oral Polio Vaccine) is adopted worldwide.

1951 *The Catcher in the Rye* by J D Salinger is published.

1952 In Helsinki, Czechoslovakian Emil Zátopek sets Olympic records in the 5,000m, 10,000m, and the marathon in which he had never run before.

1952 *Galatea of the Spheres* is painted by Salvador Dalí.

1952 *The Old Man and the Sea* by Ernest Hemmingway is published.

1952 Rosalind Franklin produces X-ray diffraction images of DNA.

1953 James Watson and Francis Crick discover the double helix structure for DNA.

1953 *En attendant Godot* (Waiting for Godot) by Samuel Beckett, premières in the Théâtre de Babylone in Paris.

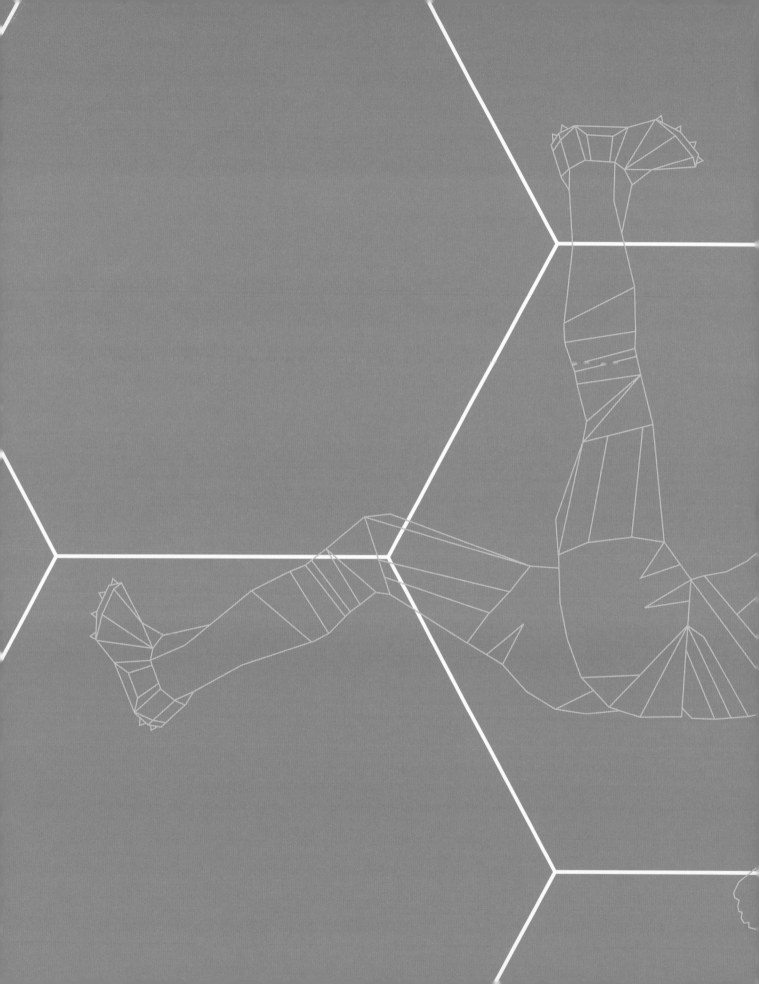

1955   In Alabama, Rosa Parks refuses to
        obey a bus driver's order to give up
        her seat for a white passenger.

1955   Einstein and Bertrand Russell sign a manifesto
        highlighting the danger posed by nuclear
        weapons. Three years later Linus Pauling
        presents the United Nations with a petition
        signed by more than 11,000 scientists calling
        for an end to nuclear weapon testing.

1957   *That'll be the day* by Buddy Holly
        is released.

1957   Pelé makes his debut with Santos
        and Brazil wins the World Cup the
        following year.

1957   The space race begins with Sputnik 1
        launched into an elliptical low Earth orbit.

1958   *Things Fall Apart* by Nigerian Chinua
        Achebe is published. The title is taken
        from a line in a W B Yeats poem: *Things fall
        apart; the centre cannot hold;*

1958   The first integrated circuits
        – the basis of all modern computer
        chips – are fabricated.

1959   Richard Feynman proposes the
        possibility of nano-scale machines.

1959   The Guggenheim Museum, designed
        by Frank Lloyd Wright opens in
        New York.

1960   *To Kill a Mockingbird* by Harper Lee is published.

1960   Harry Ferguson designs the world's
        first 4 wheel-drive Formula 1 car in
        which Stirling Moss wins the Gold
        Cup the following year.

1960   In Sri Lanka, Sirimavo Bandaranaike becomes
        the world's first female prime minister.

1962 *Silent Spring* by Rachel Carson is published.

1965 Mao Zedong starts the Cultural Revolution in China.

1962 *A Clockwork Orange* by Anthony Burgess is published.

1960 Pulses of light are produced from a pink-ruby crystal – the laser is born.

1960 In Rome, 400 athletes from 23 countries compete in the Parallel Olympics, the first Paralympics.

1961 Cosmonaut Yuri Gagarin is the first human to journey into outer space, when his Vostok spacecraft completes an orbit of the Earth on 12 April in 1961.

1963 Edward Lorenz publishes his discovery of the 'butterfly effect', significant in the development of chaos theory.

1963 'I have a Dream' - Martin Luther King speaks from the steps of the Lincoln Memorial.

1960 *La Dolce Vita* directed by Federico Fellini is released.

1962 Andy Warhol creates the silkscreen *Marilyn Diptych*.

1962 The Beatles first single, *Love Me Do*, is released.

1962 *Dr No*, the first Bond film is released.

1969 NEIL ARMSTRONG THE FIRST MAN TO WALK ON THE MOON.

2001: A SPACE ODYSSEY DIRECTED BY STANLEY KUBRICK IS RELEASED. 1968

1967 PULSARS, ROTATING NEUTRON STARS, ARE FIRST DETECTED.

1967 ARGENTINIAN MARXIST REVOLUTIONARY CHE GUEVARA IS EXECUTED IN BOLIVIA.

1969 WOODSTOCK MUSIC FESTIVAL IS HELD AT A DAIRY FARM IN THE CATSKILLS NEAR THE TOWN OF BETHEL, NE

1968 CHRISTIAAN BARNARD PER FOR FOR TRANS-AMAZONIA

1970 // Kraftwerk Electronic Music Project is formed by Ralf Hütter and Florian Schneider.

1970 // The Caspian tiger becomes extinct.

1970 // The World Series of poker begins in Las Vegas.

1971 // In Switzerland women are given the right to vote in federal elections and stand for parliament for the first time.

1972 // The first patent for an MRI machine is issued.

1972 // The *Magnavox Odyssey* is released - the first home video game console that can be connected to a TV set.

1972 // Lou Reed's song *Walk on the Wild Side* is included in his second solo album *Transformer*.

1973 // The first call is made on a hand held mobile phone (in a non-vehicle setting) using microwave technology.

1973 // Alexandr Solzhenitsyn's *The Gulag Archipelago*, based on his experiences in a Soviet forced labour camp, is published in the West.

1973 // The Sydney Opera House is completed.

1974 // The first transgenic mammal is created by integrating DNA from the SV40 virus into the genome of mice.

1974 // The Terracotta Army is discovered near the Mausoleum of the First Qin Emperor.

1975 Borobudur, a 9th-century Mahayana Buddhist Temple in Indonesia, is restored.

1975 *Bohemian Rhapsody* is recorded by Queen.

1975 *The Periodic Table* by Primo Levi is published.

1975 Mandlebrot introduces the term 'fractal'.

1977 The first photograph of the Earth and moon together in space is taken by the *Voyager 1* probe.

1977 Organisms whose life is based on chemosynthesis, rather than photosynthesis, are discovered living around the deep sea vents of the Galápagos Islands

1977 Wangari Maathai

Tschüß.

establishes the *Green Belt Movement* in Kenya. She becomes the first African woman to receive the Nobel Peace Prize in 2004.

1977 Smallpox is eradicated due to vaccination.

1978 The Rock-Hewn Churches, Lalibela, in Ethiopia are listed as a UNESCO World Heritage Site.

1978 Polish woman, Chojnowska-Liskiewicz, is the first woman to sail single-handed around the world.

1978 The first successful human birth as a result of in-vitro fertilisation.

1978 Volkswagen manufactures its last Beetle.

1981 A man working on a malfunctioning robot at a car manufacturing plant in Japan is killed when the robot's arm pushes him into a grinding machine.

1981 Superstring theory is first proposed.

1982 The film *Blade Runner* based on Philip K Dick's novel *Do Androids Dream of Electric Sheep?* is released.

1984 The first TED conference is launched to brainstorm the powerful convergence between Technology, Entertainment and Design.

1985 A hole in the ozone layer over Antarctica is identified.

1985 The Australian government returns ownership of *Uluru* (Ayres Rock) to the local Pitjantjatjara Aboriginal people.

1982 The Internet protocol suite (TCP/IP) is standardised enabling the concept of a world-wide network to develop.

1982 *Elk Cloner* is one of the first known microcomputer viruses to spread 'in the wild' via floppy disc.

1984 *L'Insoutenable légèreté de l'être* (The Unbearable Lightness of Being) by Milan Kundera is first published in a French translation. The original Czech text is published the following year.

1985 Buckminsterfullerene, a spherical allotrope of carbon, is discovered.

1985 Andy Warhol creates the *Reigning Queen* series – portraits of the queens of Denmark, Swaziland, the Netherlands and Britain.

1981 *Shergar* wins the Epsom Derby by a record 10 lengths, the longest winning margin in the race's 226-year history. Two years later *Shergar* is kidnapped but the body is never recovered.

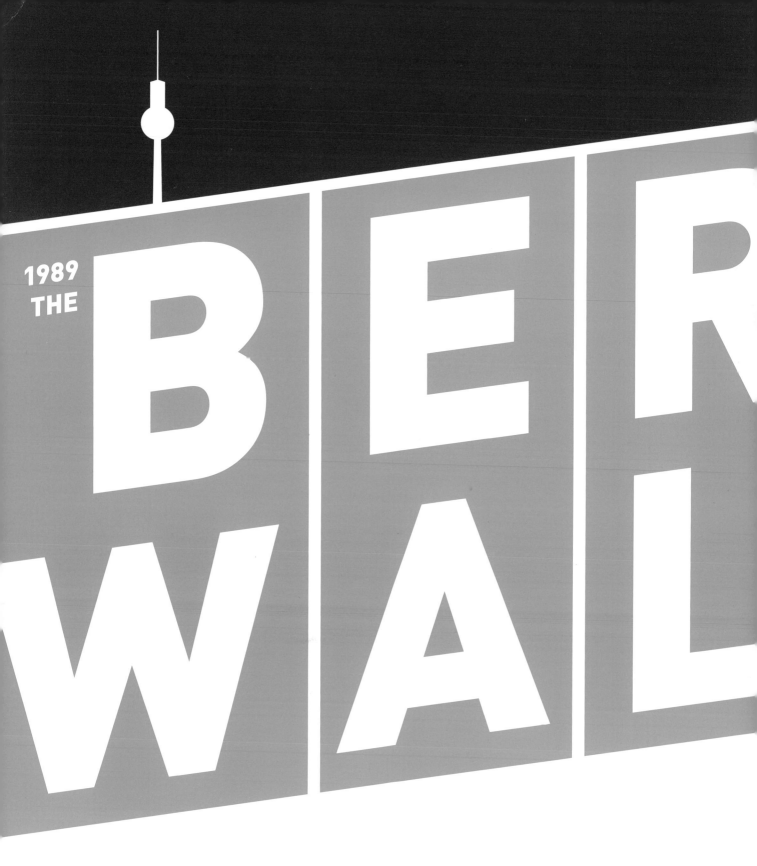

1989
THE

BER

WAL

RLIN

N

COMES DOWN.

1985–1990

1986 MARADONA SCORES THE 'HAND OF GOD' GOAL DURING THE 2–1 VICTORY FOR ARGENTINA OVER ENGLAND IN THE QUARTER FINAL OF THE WORLD CUP. 1986 *GRACELAND* BY PAUL SIMON FEATURING LADYSMITH BLACK MAMBAZO IS RELEASED. 1986 NIGERIAN WOLE SOYINKA BECOMES THE FIRST PERSON FROM THE CONTINENT OF AFRICA TO RECEIVE THE NOBEL PRIZE IN LITERATURE. 1987 GÖDEL'S ONTOLOGICAL PROOF OF THE EXISTENCE OF GOD IS PUBLISHED POSTHUMOUSLY. 1987 THE 'MITOCHONDRIAL EVE' HYPOTHESIS IS PROPOSED: ALL LIVING HUMANS ARE DESCENDED FROM ONE WOMAN. 1987 A HIGH-SPEED TRAIN SYSTEM IN JAPAN IS BASED ON THE MATHEMATICS OF FUZZY LOGIC. 1988 THE MORRIS WORM IS RELEASED ON THE INTERNET AND RESULTS IN THE FIRST CONVICTION IN THE US UNDER THE COMPUTER FRAUD AND ABUSE ACT. 1988 *NORA: THE REAL LIFE OF MOLLY BLOOM* BY BRENDA MADDOX IS PUBLISHED. 1988 TABLE TENNIS BECOMES AN OLYMPIC SPORT. 1989 THE FIRST EPISODE OF *THE SIMPSONS* IS BROADCAST. 1990 NELSON MANDELA IS FREED FROM PRISON AFTER SERVING 27 YEARS.

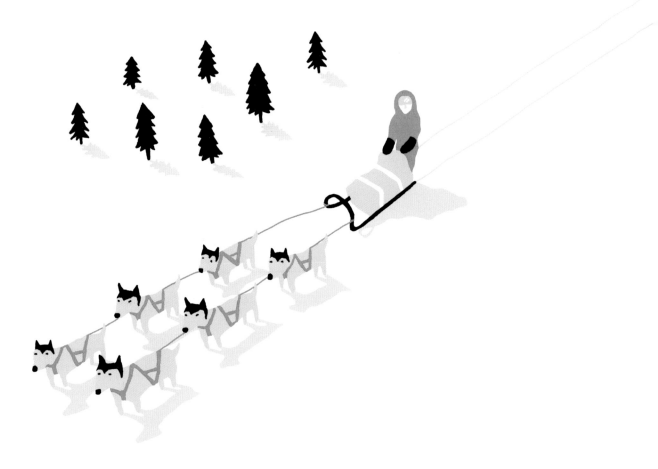

1990 The first dog sled crossing of Antarctica is completed.

1990 A team of divers off the coast of Alexandria discover stone blocks from the Pharos Lighthouse, one of the lost Seven Wonders of the ancient world. They also find the submerged ruins of Cleopatra's palace and temple complex. **1990** Hubble, the first optical based space telescope, is launched into orbit. **1991** The World Wide Web is launched at CERN. **1991** The Pretty Good Privacy (PGP) data encryption program is written and becomes the first widely available program implementing public-key cryptography. **1992** More than 100 world leaders meet in Rio de Janeiro for the first international Earth Summit. **1992** The cosmic microwave background is observed, supporting Lemaître's *Big Bang Theory* of 1929. **1994** *Knowledge of Angels* by Jill Paton Walsh is published. The plot is based on a true story about a feral woman found in France in 1731, the Maid of Châlons. **1994** South Africa holds its first universal elections and Nelson Mandela is inaugurated as president. South Africa wins the Rugby World Cup the following year. **1995** Marie Curie becomes the first woman to be entombed on her own merit in the Panthéon in Paris. **1995** *Longitude* by Dava Sobel is published. **1995** Wolves are reintroduced to Yellowstone National Park.

1995 Barings Bank, the oldest merchant bank in London, collapses. 199
1997 China regains control of Hong Kong after 99 years of British rule. 1
1997 *Deep Blue*, a chess-playing computer, wins a six-game match against worl
1998 A 40-million-year-old preserved lizard is found in a lump of amber in Gdansk, Poland
that took place between Danish atomic physicist Niels Bohr and German theoretical p.
off the coast of Namibia. It has cells large enough (max 0.75mm) to be visible to the nak
Melissa virus. 1999 Cueva de las Manos (Cave of Hands) in Argentina is listed as a UNE
the bone-made pipes used for spraying the 'paint' on the rock walls to create sil

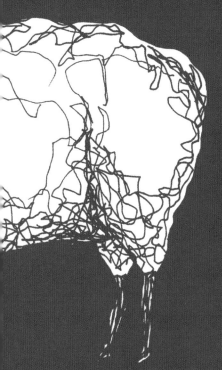

lly the sheep, the first mammal to be cloned from an adult cell, is born.
Quantum bit (qubit) teleportation is demonstrated at Innsbruck, Austria.
ampion Garry Kasparov. 1997 The Guggenheim Museum in Bilbao is completed.
98 The play *Copenhagen* by Michael Frayn debuts in London. The plot is based on a meeting
ist Werner Heisenberg in 1941. 1998 The bacterium *thiomargarita namibiensis* is found
ye. 1999 E-mail systems across the world become congested due to propagation of the
World Heritage Site. The age of the paintings (c7350 BC) is dated from the remains of
ttes of hands. 1999 Nunavut in Canada becomes a self-governing Inuit territory.

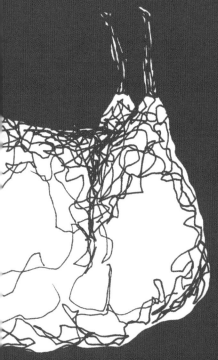

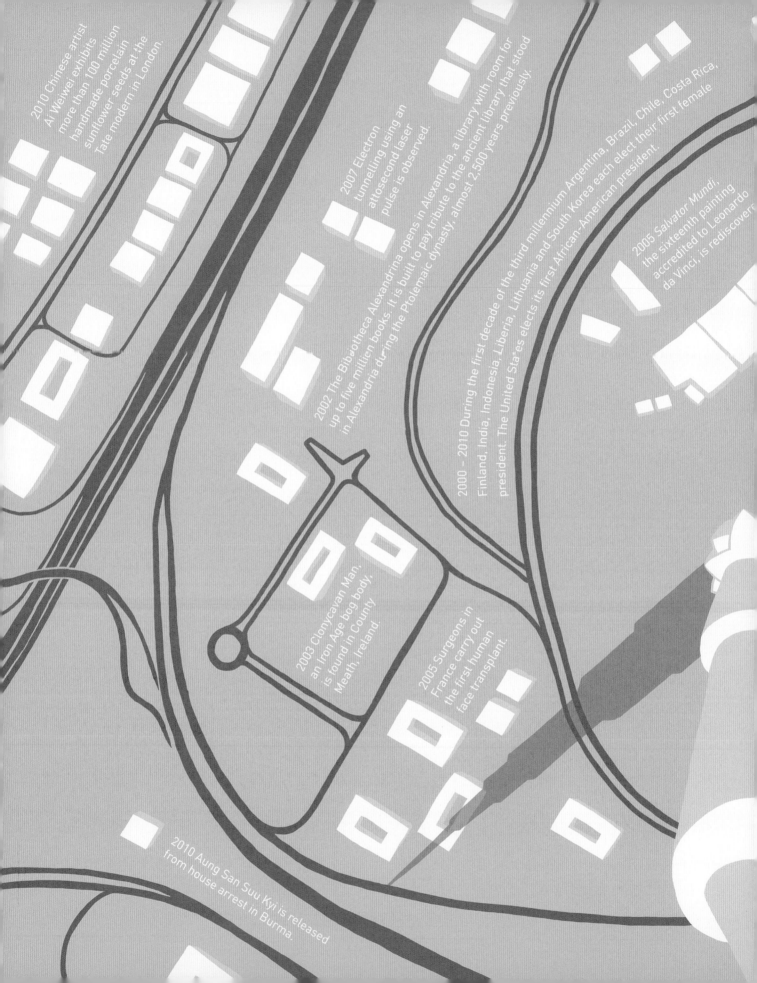

2010 Chinese artist Ai Weiwei exhibits more than 100 million handmade porcelain sunflower seeds at the Tate modern in London.

2007 Electron tunnelling using an attosecond laser pulse is observed.

2002 The Bibliotheca Alexandrina opens in Alexandria, a library with room for up to five million books. It is built to pay tribute to the ancient library that stood in Alexandria during the Ptolemaic dynasty, almost 2,500 years previously.

2000 – 2010 During the first decade of the third millennium Argentina, Brazil, Chile, Costa Rica, Finland, India, Indonesia, Liberia, Lithuania and South Korea each elect their first female president. The United States elects its first African-American president.

2005 Salvator Mundi, the sixteenth painting accredited to Leonardo da Vinci, is rediscovered.

2003 Clonycavan Man, an Iron Age bog body, is found in County Meath, Ireland.

2005 Surgeons in France carry out the first human face transplant.

2010 Aung San Suu Kyi is released from house arrest in Burma.

2000 Pope John Paul II issues a formal apology on behalf of the Catholic Church for the trial of Galileo.

2003 Complete expression of the human genome is revealed.

2001 Wikipedia, an open source online encyclopedia, is launched.

2010 The world's tallest man-made structure, the 829.8m Burj Khalifa in Dubai, United Arab Emirates is completed.

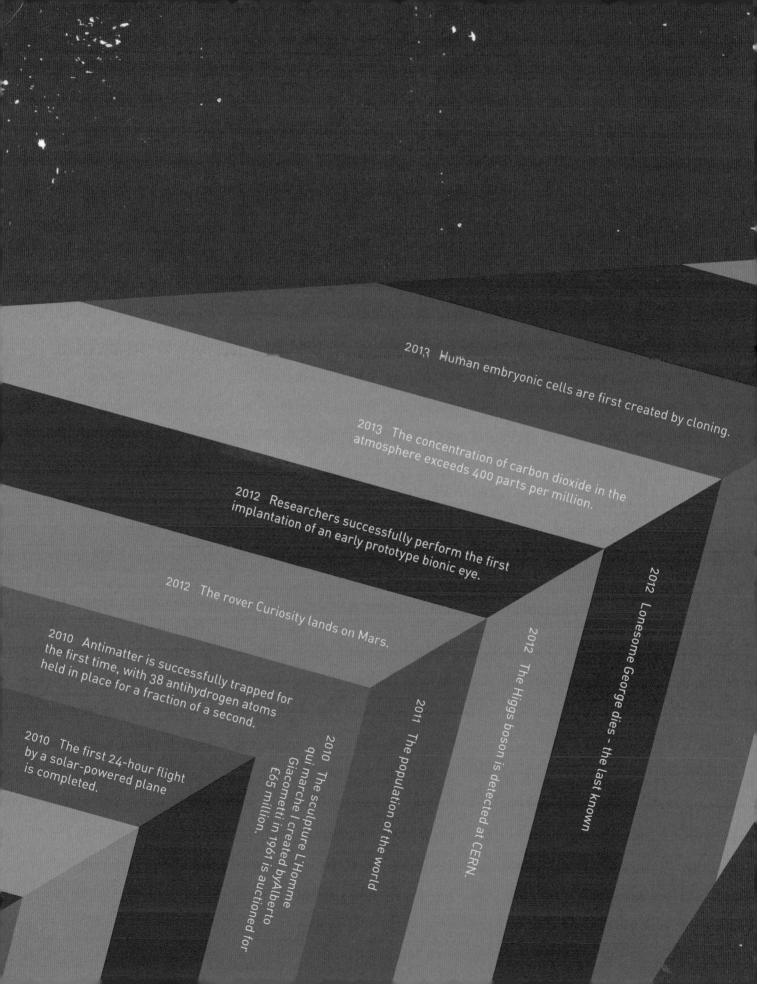

2013   Human embryonic cells are first created by cloning.

2013   The concentration of carbon dioxide in the atmosphere exceeds 400 parts per million.

2012   Researchers successfully perform the first implantation of an early prototype bionic eye.

2012   The rover Curiosity lands on Mars.

2010   Antimatter is successfully trapped for the first time, with 38 antihydrogen atoms held in place for a fraction of a second.

2010   The first 24-hour flight by a solar-powered plane is completed.

2010   The sculpture L'Homme qui marche I created byAlberto Giacometti in 1961 is auctioned for £65 million.

2011   The population of the world

2012   The Higgs boson is detected at CERN.

2012   Lonesome George dies – the last known

2013   The Voyager probe, launched in 1977, reaches almost 19 billion kilometres from Earth and becomes the first man made object to leave the solar system.

1400-1500

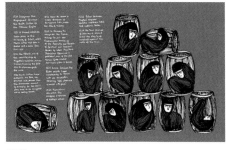

1500

1505

1513

1520

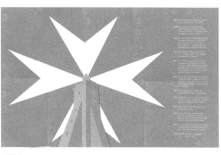

1528

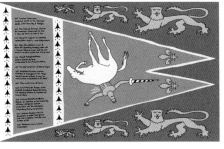

1535

1540

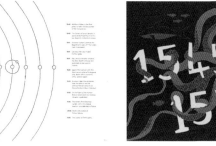

1545

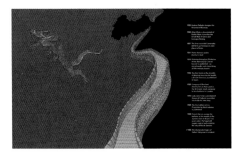

1550

1555

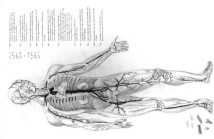

1560

1565

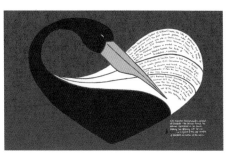

1570

1575

1580

1585

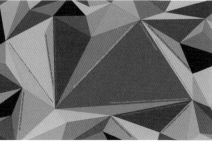

1590

1595

1600

1605

1610

1615

1620

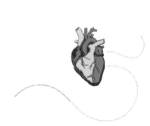

1625

1630

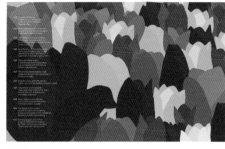

1635

1640

1645

1650

1655

1660

1665

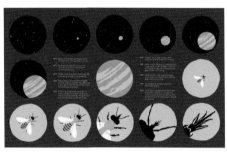

1670

1675

1680

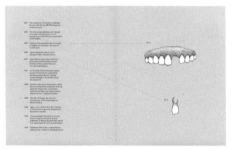

1685

1690

1695

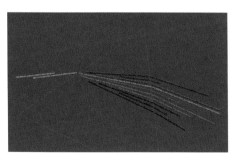

1700

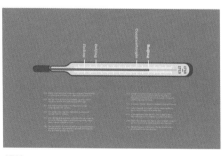

1705

1710

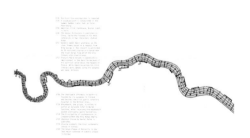

1715

1720

1725

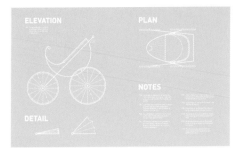

1730

1735

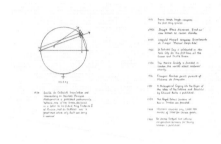

1740

1745

1750

1755

1760

1765

1770

1775

1780

1785

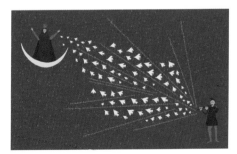

1790

1795

1800

1805

1810

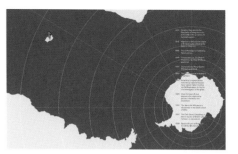

1815

1820

1825

1830

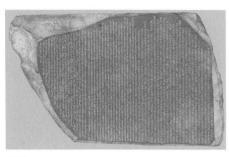

1835

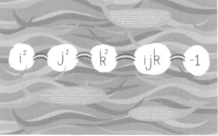

1840

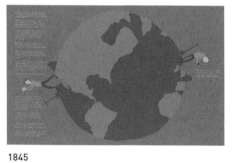

1845

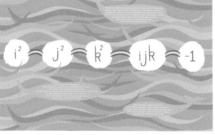

1850

1855

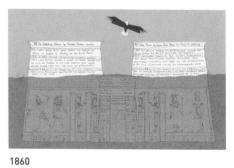

1860

1865

1870

1875

1880

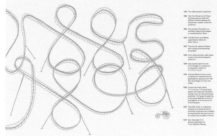

1885

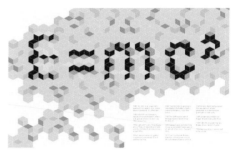

1890

1895

1900

1905

1910

1915

1925 herbert bayer
develops the designs
for universal lettering
for the bauhaus
letterhead

1920

1925

1930

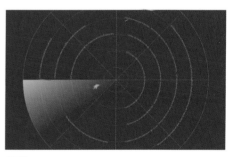

1935

1940

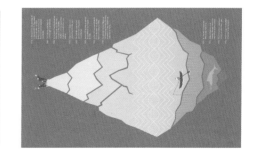

1945

1950

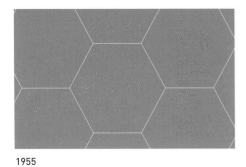

1955

1960

1965

1970

1975

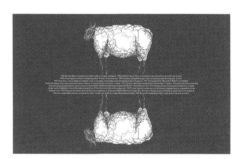

1980

1985

1990

2000

2010

1995

1400 – 2013

1420	Construction of the Chinese Forbidden City is completed in Beijing.
c1424	*Palazzo Ducale* (the Doge's Palace) is completed in Venice.
c1425	Packs of playing cards are among the most popular products of Europe's first printing presses.
1429	Joan of Arc ends the Siege of Orléans and turns the tide of the Hundred Years' War. She is burned at the stake two years later at the age of 19.
c1440	Johannes Gutenberg invents the printing press with moveable type.
c1450	The construction of Machu Picchu is completed.
1457	Golf is banned by King James II of Scotland who feels it is distracting young men from archery practice.
1469	Lorenzo de' Medici takes power in Florence.
1485	Botticelli paints *Birth of Venus*.
1492	Christopher Columbus arrives at an island in the Bahamas archipelago that he names *La Isla Española*, now known as Haiti and the Dominican Republic.
1498	Vasco da Gama commands the first fleet of ships to sail from Europe to India.
1498	Leonardo da Vinci completes *The Last Supper*.
c1500	Johannes Trithemius writes *Steganographia* (hidden writing) a treatise on cryptography and steganography disguised as a book on magic.
1500	Johannes Werner in Nuremberg, Germany tracks a comet taking observations between 1st and 24th June.
1500	In Rome Nicolaus Copernicus observes a lunar eclipse.
1502	Portuguese navigator João da Nova discovers the island of Saint Helena.
1503	Pope Alexander VI, Roderic Llançol i de Borja dies.
1503	Michel de Nostredame (Nostradamus) is born in France.
1503	Spanish forces defeat the French in the Battle of Cerignola - considered to be the first battle won by gunpowder and small arms.
c1504	Michelangelo creates the sculpture of *David*.
c1505	Leonardo da Vinci paints the *Mona Lisa*.
c1505	Peter Henlein uses iron parts and coiled springs to start building the first portable timepieces, later known as 'Nuremberg Eggs'.
c1505	Leonardo da Vinci produces the *Codex on the Flight of Birds*.
1507	Dürer completes his painting *Adam and Eve*.
1507	Explorer Amerigo Vespucci establishes that the New World is a separate land mass. A pamphlet wrongly describes him as its discoverer and America acquires its name.
1509	*De Divina Proportione* by Pacioli is published (illustrated by da Vinci). The first part studies and describes the golden ratio.
1509	Erasmus writes *In Praise of Folly*, a satirical attack on the traditions of European society, the Catholic Church and popular superstitions.
1509	Raphael creates frescos for the papal apartments in the Vatican.
1510	The first known influenza pandemic originates in Asia.
1510	The Portuguese conquer Goa and it becomes the capital of their Asian maritime empire.
1512	Michelangelo completes the ceiling of the Sistine Chapel.

1512	Hieronymus Brunschwig publishes *Big Book of Distillation*, describing medicinal herbs and the construction of stills for processing them.
1513	Niccolò Machiavelli writes *The Prince*.
1513	Johannes Stoffler's treatise on the construction and use of astrolabes is published.
1515	An Indian rhinoceros arrives in Lisbon, the first to be seen in Europe since Roman times.
1515	Albrecht Dürer creates a woodcut of a rhinoceros from a written description and sketch by another artist, without ever seeing the animal himself.
c1515	The world's first floating assembly line is established at the Arsenale in Venice.
1516	The fictional island of *Utopia* is described by Thomas Moore.
1516	Titian completes the *Assumption of the Virgin*, his first major commission in Venice.
1517	Martin Luther posts his *Ninety-Five Theses*, leading to the Reformation.
1519	The fall of Moctezuma II ends the Aztec empire.
1520	Portuguese explorer Ferdinand Magellan becomes the first European to sight Chile as he sails through the straits between South America and Tierra del Fuego.
1520	Suleyman the Magnificent becomes the tenth Sultan of the Ottoman Empire.
1521	A student rebellion takes place in the University of Erfurt where Martin Luther had been a student and a monk from 1501 – 1511.
1522	The *Vittoria*, one of the surviving ships of Magellan's expedition, returns to Spain, becoming the first ship to circumnavigate the world.
1523	Martin Luther helps Katharina von Bora, his eventual wife, escape from the Nimbschen convent by arranging for her and 11 other nuns to be smuggled out in herring barrels.
1524	Vasco da Gama is made Governor of Portuguese India, under the title of Viceroy.
1525	In Germany the pamphlet *The Twelve Articles: The Just and Fundamental Articles of All the Peasantry and Tenants of Spiritual and Temporal Powers by Whom They Think Themselves Oppressed* is published, one of the first human rights related documents written in Europe.
1525	Lucas Cranach the Elder paints *Cupid complaining to Venus* with an inscription observing 'life's pleasure is mixed with pain.'
1525	Paracelsus discovers the analgesic properties of diethyl ether.
1526	Babur becomes Mughal emperor, invades northern India, and captures Delhi.
1527	The Town Statutes of Galway in Ireland forbid the playing of handball against the walls of the town.
1528	The Maya peoples drive the Spanish Conquistadores out of Yucatán.
c1528	The Gardens of Babur in Kabul, Afghanistan are created and later become the final resting place of the first Mughal emperor Babur.
1529	Occultist Heinrich Cornelius Agrippa publishes *Declamatio de nobilitate et praecellentia foeminei sexus* (Declamation on the Nobility and Pre-eminence of the Female Sex).
1530	The Knights of Malta are formed when Malta is given to the Knights Hospitaller by Charles V.

1530 The first book devoted to dentistry is published in Germany: *Artzney büchlein: wider allerlei kranckeyten und gebrechen der tzeen (The little medicinal book for all kinds of diseases and infirmities of the teeth).*

1531 One of the earliest lighthouses in the world, the Kõpu Lighthouse on the Estonian island of Hiiumaa, is first lit. It remains in continuous use into the 21st century.

1532 Francisco Pizarro defeats and captures Inca emperor Atahualpa.

1532 Henry VIII builds a court for the game of Royal Tennis, now known as Real Tennis, at Hampton Court Palace.

1533 Hans Holbein the Younger paints *The Ambassadors.*

1534 Explorer Jacques Cartier claims the area now known as Quebec, for France, describing it as Kanata, the Huron-Iroquois word for village.

1535 Jacopo Berengario da Carpi publishes *Anatomia Carpi,* the first anatomical text with illustrations, in Bologna.

1535 Lima is founded as la Ciudad de los Reyes, City of Kings.

1535 Fray Tomás de Berlanga discovers the Galapagos Islands when his boat is blown off course en route to Peru.

1535 Leonhart Fuchs grows medicinal plants in the botanical garden of the University of Tübingen.

1536 Henry VIII is injured in a jousting accident from which he never fully recovers.

1536 Adam Ries publishes a book of tables for calculating everyday prices with a foreward noting his concern 'that the poor common man not be cheated when buying bread.'

1537 Niccolò Tartaglia publishes *La Nova Scientia* applying mathematics to the study of ballistics.

1537 The reign of Cosimo I de' Medici begins.

1538 Hans Holbein the Younger paints portraits of potential Queens for Henry VIII including Christina of Denmark and Anne of Cleves.

1538 Maddalena Casulana composes *First Book of Madrigals for Four Voices* - the first female composer to have her music printed and published in the West.

1538 Titian paints *Venus of Urbino.*

1539 Johannes Baptista Montanus, Professor of Medicine at the University of Padua, introduces bedside examination into the curriculum, integrating theory and practice.

1540 Ethiopian musical notation is developed.

1540 Andreas Vesalius shows in dissections in public that female and male skeletons have the same number of ribs.

1540 Waltham Abbey is the final priory to fall in the dissolution of the monasteries.

1540 The Society of Jesus (Jesuits) is approved by Pope Paul III, in his bull *Regimini militantis Ecclesiae.*

1541 Ottoman Sultan Suleiman the Magnificent seals off The Golden Gate in Jerusalem.

1541 Gerardus Mercator makes his first globe.

1541 Elia Levita's chivalric romance, the *Bovo-Bukh,* is the earliest published secular work in Yiddish.

1543 Japan's first contact with the West occurs when a Portuguese ship, blown off its course to China, lands in Japan.

1543 Nicolaus Copernicus proposes that the earth is not the centre of the Universe in *De Revolutionibus Orbium Celestium.*

1543 *On the Fabric of the Human Body in Seven books* by Andreas Vesalius is published.

1545 The world's first Botanical Garden, still in its original location, is established in Padua.

c1545 Silver is discovered at Potosí, Bolivia.

1545 The Council of Trent opens.

c1545 Il Bronzino paints *Venus, Cupid, Folly and Time.*

1545 In China, failure of the harvest in the Henan province causes famine.

c1546 *The sea monk* is the name given to a sea animal found off the eastern coast of the Danish island of Zealand. Many now believe this to have been the giant squid *Architeuthis.*

1546 A Persian miniature made during the Safavid dynasty shows Persian courtiers on horseback playing a game of polo.

1546 Girolamo Fracastoro proposes that epidemic diseases are caused by transferable tiny particles or 'spores' that can transmit infection by direct or indirect contact.

1547 Ivan IV (Ivan the Terrible) is the first person to be crowned as Tsar of All the Russias.

1547 In Malaysia, Francis Xavier, one of the first seven Jesuits and student of Ignatius of Loyola, meets a Japanese man named Anjirō who becomes the first Japanese Christian.

1548 The Ming Dynasty government of China issues a decree banning all foreign trade and closes down all seaports along the coast.

1548 Firearms are used for the first time on the battlefield in Japan.

1549 The spire of Lincoln Cathedral in England is blown down, leaving St. Olaf's Church, Tallinn, in Estonia as the world's tallest structure (125m) until 1625.

1550 The laying out of the gardens at the Villa d'Este in Tivoli begins.

1550 Andrea Palladio designs the *Rotunda* in Vincenza.

1550 Altan Khan, a descendant of Kublai Khan, breaches the Great Wall of China and besieges Beijing.

1551 The first recorded Commedia dell'Arte performances take place in Rome.

1551 Pieter Aertsen paints *Butcher's Stall.*

1551 *Historiae Animalium* (Histories of the Animals) by Conrad Gesner is published - an encyclopedic work describing all the animals known.

1553 The first book on the benefits of physical exercise for health, *Libro del Exercicio,* is published in Spain.

1553 *Company of Merchant Adventurers to New Lands* is the first joint-stock company to be chartered in London.

1553 Lady Jane Grey is proclaimed Queen of England, a position she holds for nine days.

1555 The first edition of *Les Propheties* by Nostradamus is published.

1555 French forces occupy the harbour at the mouth of the Janeiro river in Brazil. Two years later, Portugal will regain control and establish the city of Rio de Janeiro.

c1555 The illuminated tugra of Sultan Suleyman is created.

1556 Guillaume Rondelet's anatomical drawing of a sea urchin is the earliest extant depiction of an invertebrate.

1556	Akbar the Great becomes the third Mughal Emperor at the age of 13.
1556	The first printing press in India is introduced at Saint Paul's College in Goa.
1556	Phillip II becomes King of Spain. During his reign Spanish colonies, including the Philippine Islands, are claimed in all the known continents.
1557	Spain becomes bankrupt, throwing German banking houses into chaos.
1557	German adventurer Hans Staden publishes an account of his detention by the Tupí people of Brazil - *True Story and Description of a Country of Wild, Naked, Grim, Man-eating People in the New World, America.*
1557	At the Battle of St. Quentin French surgeon Ambroise Paré notes that maggots assist in the healing of wounds.
1558	*Magia Naturalis* (Natural Magic), a work of popular science by Giambattista della Porta, is published in Naples.
1559	Lorenzo Valla's book of 1440 which exposed the fact that the Donation of Constantine was a forgery, is placed on the *Index Librorum Prohibitorum.*
1559	Jean Nicot describes the medicinal properties of tobacco and introduces it in the form of snuff to the French court.
c1559	John Shakespeare (father of the playwright) whitewashes over the religious frescoes in the Guild Chapel of the Holy Cross in Stratford-upon-Avon following the royal injunction calling for all 'superstition and idolatry' be removed from places of worship.
1560	The oldest surviving violin (dated inside), known as the *Charles IX*, is made in Cremona, in northern Italy.
1560	Building of the *Uffizi* palace in Florence commences. It is designed by Giorgio Vasari for Cosimo I de' Medici as the offices for the Florentine magistrates.
1561	Ruy López de Segura describes new techniques for playing chess in his publication *Book of the Liberal Invention and Art of the Game Chess.*
1562	Fray Diego de Landa, the acting Bishop of Yucatán, burns the sacred books of the Maya.
1562	Giacomo Barozzi da Vignola publishes *Rules of the Five Orders of Architecture.*
c1563	*Tower of Babel* is painted by Pieter Breugel the Elder.
1563	Garcia de Orta publishes *Colóquios dos Simples e Drogas da India* in Goa, the first text in a Western language on tropical medicine and drugs, including a classic description of cholera.
1564	Ivan Fyodorov and Pyotr Mstislavets establish the Moscow Print Yard and start to publish works using moveable type. Persecuted for this by the traditional Muscovite scribes they are forced to flee to the Grand Duchy of Lithuania after their printing workshop is burned down.
1564	Michelangelo dies. Galileo is born. Shakespeare is born.
1564	An early form of the pencil is invented when a huge graphite mine is discovered in Borrowdale, Cumbria, England.
1564	Authors and printers are excommunicated if they print any works from the list of prohibited books.

c1564	Naples prohibits kissing in public under penalty of death.
1565	The College of Physicians of London is empowered to carry out human dissections.
1565	The first Martello tower, the Torra di Mortella is completed as part of the Genovese defence system in Upper Corsica.
1566	Calvinists destroy many religious works of art in Belgium, the Netherlands, and Luxembourg.
1566	The Spanish doubloon is first minted during the reign of Philip II of Spain.
1566	Pope Pius V orders the expulsion of prostitutes from Rome.
1566	The Ottomans build the first bridge to cross the Neretva river at Mostar (Bosnia-Herzegovina). The reconstructed bridge is now known as *Stari Most* (Old Bridge).
1566	Danish astronomer Tycho Brahe loses part of his nose in a sword duel due to a quarrel over the legitimacy of a mathematical formula.
1567	1,200 watchtowers are constructed on the Great Wall of China in order to warn of approaching Mongol raiders.
1569	The first recorded lottery in England is performed at the west door of St Paul's Cathedral. Each share costs ten shillings and the proceeds are used for public works such as repairing harbours.
1569	The Bible is printed in Castilian for the first time.
1569	*The Mercator projection*, a cylindrical map projection created by the Flemish geographer and cartographer Gerardus Mercator, is published.
c1570	Giuseppe Arcimboldo paints *The Librarian.*
1570	John Shakespeare (father of William) seeks the title of gentleman and applies for his coat-of-arms.
1570	Andrea Palladio's treatise, *Four Books of Architecture*, is published.
1570	*Theatrum Orbis Terrarum* (Theatre of the World) by Abraham Ortelius is printed - an early modern atlas.
1572	Vilcabamba in Peru, the last independent remnant of the Inca Empire, is conquered by Spain.
1572	Cornelius Gemma is the first European to observe and record an illustration of a Supernova (in the constellation Cassiopeia).
1572	Raphael Bombelli calculates using imaginary numbers.
1573	The first Spanish galleon laden with silver to trade in exchange for porcelain and silk in China, lands at Manila in the Philippines.
1573	The Muromachi period ends when the 15th and last shogun of this line, Ashikaga Yoshiaki, is driven out of the capital in Kyoto by Oda Nobunaga.
1574	*La Alameda* in Seville, Spain is laid out as Europe's first public garden.
1575	Nicholas Hilliard paints a portrait of Elizabeth I the *Pelican Portrait*. The pelican represented on her brooch, feeding her offspring with her own blood, is a symbol of the self-sacrifice of Elizabeth as mother of the nation.
c1575	Jacopo Tintoretto paints *The Origin of the Milky Way.*
1575	Ambroise Paré, the father of modern surgery, writes 'There are five duties of surgery: to remove what is superfluous, to restore what has been dislocated, to separate what has grown together, to reunite what has been divided, and to redress the defects of nature.'
1576	James Burbage builds *The Theatre,* the first permanent public playhouse in London.
1577	Building begins on Tycho Brahe's observatory called Uraniborg (heavenly castle) on the island of Hven in the Danish Sound.
1578	Sonam Gyrso becomes the first officially recognized Dalai Lama of Tibet.
1579	Giambologna begins his sculpture, the *Rape of the Sabine Women.*
1579	Francis Drake lands in North California and gives the name Nova Albion (New England) to the region of the Pacific coast that he claims for England.
1580	The Ostrog Bible, the first complete Bible printed in a Slavic language, is published.

1580   The Istanbul observatory Taqi al-Din is destroyed by Sultan Selim II.

1580   A broadside ballad is registered at the London Stationers' Company with the title *A Newe Northen Dittye of ye Ladye Greene Sleves.*

1580   The *concerto delle donne*, a group of professional female singers, is founded by Alfonso II, Duke of Ferrara.

1580   The first session of the Jewish *Vaad* (Council of Four Lands) is held in Lublin, Poland.

1581   The Ming Dynasty Chancellor of China imposes the *Single Whip Reform*, in which taxes (to be paid in silver) are assessed on properties recorded in the land census.

1582   Italy, Poland-Lithuania, Portugal, and Spain become the first countries to change from the Julian to the Gregorian calendar, skipping 11 days (Thursday 4th October is followed by Friday 15th Oct.)

1582   John Dee becomes a recognized expert in mathematics, astronomy and navigation while also practicing the art of scrying - looking into a translucent ball or crystal to see spiritual visions.

1583   Carolus Clusius publishes the first book on Alpine flora.

c1583   Lavinia Fontana paints *Newborn Baby in a Crib*. Despite bearing eleven children she continues to paint to support the family while her husband serves as her assistant.

1584   The Jesuit China missionary, Matteo Ricci produces the first European-style map of the world in Chinese now known as 'the impossible black tulip of cartography' as no prints of the map survive.

c1585   A portrait is painted of Christopher Marlowe with the motto inscribed: QUOD ME NUTRIT ME DESTRUIT (that which nourishes me destroys me).

1585   Palladio's *Teatro Olimpico* in Vicenza is completed with trompe-l'œil onstage scenery to give the appearance of long streets receding to a distant horizon. It is the oldest surviving stage set still in existence.

1585   Chocolate is introduced to Europe commercially.

1585   Shakespeare's twins, Hamnet and Judith, are born.

1586   Mary Queen of Scots, the Catholic cousin of the Protestant Queen Elizabeth 1, is tried for treason.

1586   Simon Stevin, a Flemish mathematician, demonstrates that two objects of different weight fall with the same speed.

1587   Construction begins on the *Pont Neuf,* the oldest standing bridge across the Seine in Paris.

1587   The Banco della Piazza di Rialto is opened in Venice to hold merchants' funds on safe deposit and enable financial transactions to be made without the physical transfer of coins.

1588   In Japan Hideyoshi forbids ordinary peasants from owning weapons and starts a sword hunt to confiscate arms. The swords are melted down to create a statue of the Buddha.

1588   With the Spanish Armada in sight Queen Elizabeth I rallies her troops with the words 'I know I have the body but of a weak and feeble woman; but I have the heart and stomach of a king.'

1589   Shakespeare writes his first play, *Comedy of Errors.*

1590   Giuseppe Arcimboldo creates a portrait of *Rudolf II as Vertumnus* (Roman God of the seasons) using fruit, vegetables and flowers in the painting.

1590   In the Netherlands, glass lenses are adapted for use in the first microscopes and telescopes.

1590   The first half of *The Fairie Queen* by Edmund Spenser is published.

1591   François Viète introduces the new algebra using letters as parameters in equations.

1591   The Rialto Bridge in Venice is completed.

1591   Morocco captures Timbuktu.

1592   Trinity College Dublin is founded.

1592   *The Spanish Tragedy, or Hieronimo is Mad Again* by Thomas Kyd is published.

1594   The first tulip bulbs planted in Holland come into flower.

1594   The first permanent anatomical theatre is opened at the University of Padua.

1594   St. Paul's College in Macau is founded by Jesuits - the first western style university in the Far East.

1594   *The Cardsharps* is painted by Caravaggio.

1595   Bartholomaeus Pitiscus introduces the term *trigonometry* to Western European languages.

1595   In the first Italian book on obstetrics Scipione Mercurio advocates caesarean operation in cases of contracted pelvis.

1597   Francis Bacon writes 'Knowledge is power' in *Meditationes Sacrae* (Sacred Meditations).

1597   In Japan, Hideyoshi has twenty-six Christians executed by public crucifixion.

1597   Galileo invents the Geometric and Military Compass – the device functions as an early mathematical calculator.

1598   *Dafne* by Jacopo Peri, the earliest known work that could be considered a modern opera, is performed during *Carnevale* in Florence.

1598   The word 'coffee' enters the English language via the Dutch word 'koffie'.

1598   In a manuscript, the Guildford Book of Court uses the word 'creckett' for a game played in Guildford school.

1599   'The evil that men do lives after them/the good is oft interred with their bones', Mark Anthony eulogises Julius Caesar in Shakespeare's play.

1599   The Globe Theatre is built in London. A flag raised over the theatre indicates the type of play being performed on any day - white for comedy, black for tragedy and red for history.

1600   The navigator William Adams is the first Englishman to reach Japan. He becomes a key advisor to *shogun* Tokugawa Ieyasu and builds Japan's first western-style ships.

1600   Laying out begins on the parterre in Castello Ruspoli, Italy.

1600   Dominican friar and astronomer Giordano Bruno is burned at the stake for proposing, amongst other things, that the Sun is a star.

c1600   Sumo wrestling becomes a spectator sport in Japan.

1601   The Jesuit, Matteo Ricci becomes the first European to enter the Forbidden City in Beijing, China.

1601   The Battle of Kinsale in Ireland.

1602   Felix Plater publishes *Praxis Medica* presenting a method for classifying diseases by their symptoms.

1602   The Confucian scholar Li Zhi is imprisoned in China for spreading the 'dangerous idea' that women are the intellectual equals of men and should be given equal opportunity in education.

1602   Caravaggio paints *The Taking of Christ.*

1602   The Dutch East India Company is formed as a joint-stock company with shares that are readily tradable.

c1604   Marie Venier is the first female actress to appear on stage in Paris.

1604   The Sikh Holy Scripture *Guru Granth Sahib* is compiled by Guru Arjan.

1604   Doctor *Faustus* by Christopher Marlowe is published. It is based on the story of *Faust,* a man who sells his soul to the devil for power and knowledge.

1605   The world's first newspaper, *Relation aller Fürnemmen und gedenckwürdigen Historien* (Collection of all Distinguished and Commemorable News) is published in Strasbourg.

1605   *Don Quixote part I* by Miguel de Cervantes is published.

1605   The plot to blow up the English Houses of Parliament is foiled when Guy Fawkes is discovered guarding 36 barrels of gunpowder in a cellar below the Parliament building.

1607   The Bank of Genoa fails after the announcement of national bankruptcy in Spain.

1607   Flight of the Earls: Hugh O'Neill and Rory O'Donnell flee Ireland heading for Spain.

1607   *Hamlet* is performed aboard the East India Company ship *Red Dragon* while anchored off the coast of Sierra Leone.

1607   Claudio Monteverdi writes *L'Orfeo,* one of the first great operas.

1609   Johannes Kepler publishes his first two laws of planetary motion in *Astronomia Nova*.

1610   Galileo constructs a refracting telescope and observes the moons of Jupiter, naming them Io, Europa, Ganymede and Callisto.

c1610   Peter Paul Rubens paints *The Massacre of the Innocents*. The work will be sold at auction at Sotheby's, London in 2002 for £49.5 million.

1610   Galileo shows the Doge of Venice how to use his refracting telescope to see ships approaching from far out at sea.

1610   Edward Coke, Chief Justice of England's Court of Common Pleas, affirms the supremacy of the common law, which limits the power of parliament as well as the king.

1610   The Portuguese colony of Brazil accumulates wealth through the production and export of up to 71,000 tons of sugar a year.

1612   Artemisia Gentileschi paints *Judith Slaying Holofernes*, a classic scene from the Bible. Gentileschi draws herself as Judith and her mentor Agostino Tassi (who was tried in court for her rape) as Holofernes.

1613   Mikhail Romanov becomes Tsar of Russia, establishing the Romanov dynasty.

1613   A locust swarm destroys La Camarque, France.

1613   Japanese shogun Tokugawa Ieyasu decrees that William Adams the pilot is dead and that samurai Miura Anjin is born.

1613   Pocahontas is captured by the English. She converts to Christianity and marries John Rolfe, a tobacco planter, in Jamestown Virginia the following year.

1614   In the last years of his life El Greco completes *The Opening of the Fifth Seal*, believed to be the prime source of inspiration for Picasso's *Les Demoiselles d'Avignon* (1907).

1615   A London armsmaster begins offering public lessons in fisticuffs to the gentry.

1616   The Sultan Ahmed Mosque in Istanbul (the Blue Mosque) is completed.

1616   *De Revolutionibus* by Copernicus is suspended until corrections are made. Galileo makes the corrections to his copy very lightly.

c1616   Astronomer Johannes Kepler is charged with witchcraft. His mother is charged with the same offence several years later.

1616   The first non-aristocratic, free public school in Europe is opened in Frascati, Italy.

1616   The first performance of the play *Christmas, His Masque* by Ben Jonson takes place. Father Christmas is dressed as a jolly figure in a comical costume suggesting that he is descended from the presenter of the medieval mid-winter festival called the 'Feast of Fools'.

1616   Moralist writer John Deacon publishes a quarto entitled Tobacco Tortured or the *Filthie Fume of Tobacco Refined*.

1616   Dutch traders smuggle the coffee plant out of Mocha, a port in Yemen on the Red Sea, and cultivate it at the Amsterdam Botanical Gardens.

1618   Ivan Petlin, a Siberian Cossack, is the first Russian to travel to China on an official mission.

1618   The Defenestration of Prague triggers the Thirty Years War.

1620   A merry-go-round is seen at a fair in Philippapolis, Turkey – one of the earliest records of a carousel at a fair.

1620   The Pilgrim Fathers arrive at Plymouth Rock on the *Mayflower*.

1620   Cornelis Drebbel builds the first navigable submarine while working for the English Royal Navy.

1620   The oldest stone church in French North America, *Notre-Dame-des-Anges*, is founded in Quebec, Canada.

1621   Willebrord Snellius van Royen describes the law of refraction later known as Snell's Law.

1622   *Congregatio de Propaganda Fide* is set up to spread the Roman Catholic faith and counter the expansion of Protestant colonization.

1623   The first American temperance law is enacted in Virginia.

1623   *Mr. William Shakespeares Comedies, Histories, & Tragedies* – the First Folio is published.

1623   *Secret History* by Procopius, written in the 6th Century, is discovered in the Vatican Library.

1623   A psychiatric treatise *Maladie d'Amour ou Mélancolie Érotique* by Jacques Ferrand is published.

1624   Portuguese Jesuit priest António de Andrade becomes the first European to enter Tibet.

1624   Ana de Sousa Nzingha Mbande becomes Queen Nzinga of Ndongo and Matamba (now Angola).

1624   Frans Hals paints the portrait now known as the *Laughing Cavalier*.

1625   Francis Bacon writes 'he that will not apply new remedies must expect new evils' in his publication *The Essayes or Counsels, Civill and Morall*.

c1625   William Oughtred invents a circular slide rule to perform multiplication and division but is involved in a priority dispute about the invention with Richard Delamain.

1625   Galileo writes about the nature of indivisible points.

1626   Peter Minuit buys Manhattan from Native Americans (thought to be the Lenape tribe) for trade goods valued at 60 guilders.

1627   The last recorded auroch, the ancestor of domestic cattle, dies in the Jaktorów Forest in Poland.

1628   The War of the Mantuan Succession begins, caused by the extinction of the direct male line of the House of Gonzaga.

1628   William Harvey describes the circulation of blood being pumped through the body by the heart.

1629   Actresses are banned in Japan.

1629   German and French troops carry the bubonic plague across the Alps into Italy.

1629   Pope Urban VIII asks Bernini to sketch possible renovations to the *Trevi Fountain*.

1629   John Parkinson publishes *Paradisi in Sole Paradisus Terrestris: a garden of all sorts of pleasant flowers which our English ayre will permit to be noursed up*.

1630   In the Mughal Empire, Shah Jahan's *Pearl Mosque* at Lahore Fort is consecrated.

1630   Pierre de Fermat studies the curve later known as the *Witch of Agnesi*.

1630   Cornelius Drebbel produces an early form of magic lantern or slide projector.

1630   Massachusetts Bay Colony outlaws the possession of cards, dice, and gaming tables.

1631   William Oughtred introduces the multiplication sign (×) and the proportion sign (::).

1631   *La Gazette*, the first French newspaper, is founded.

1631   Algerian pirates sack Baltimore in County Cork, Ireland.

1632   Construction of the Taj Mahal begins.

1632   Rembrandt paints *The Anatomy Lesson of Dr. Nicolaes Tulp*.

1633   The first Protestant cathedral to be built in Europe, St Columb's Cathedral in Derry, Ireland is completed.

1633   Galileo's banned publication *The Dialogue* increases in price from ½ scudo to 6 scudo on the black market. It is smuggled across the Alps to Strasbourg to be translated into Latin for distribution in Europe.

1634   *The Story of Stories* by Giambattista Basile is published posthumously. It includes the tale of Cenerentola and the character Zezolla – an early version of *Cinderella*.

1635   Chen Hongshou creates an ink and colour self-portrait.

1635   In Japan, all foreign commerce is confined to the artificial island of Dejima in Nagasaki Bay.

1636   King Christian of Denmark gives an order that all beggars that are able to work must be sent to Brinholmen, to build ships or to work as galley rowers.

1636   New College (Harvard University) is established as the first college to be founded in North America.

1636   John Milton and Thomas Hobbes are amongst the many supporters to visit Galileo while he is under house arrest in Italy.

1637   The first recorded European-made eyeglasses to enter China (38,421 pairs) arrive on six ships.

1637   Pierre de Fermat makes a note in a document margin about a proof that will later be known as *Fermat's Last Theorem*.

1637   René Descartes writes the phrase; *cogito ergo sum* (I am thinking, therefore I exist).

1637 Tulip Mania reaches its peak – some single tulip bulbs sell for more than 10 times the annual income of a skilled craftsman.

1638 Pedro Teixeira makes the first ascent of the Amazon River, from its mouth to Quito, Ecuador.

1638 The Beijing Gazette makes an official switch in its production process of newspapers, from woodblock printing to movable type printing.

1640 Rembrandt paints *Self Portrait at age 34,* believed to be inspired by Titian's similarly posed painting c1509 *A man with a quilted sleeve.*

1640 A form of bayonet is invented which will eventually replace the pike.

1640 Giovanna Garzoni paints *Still Life with Bowl of Citrons* tempera on vellum.

1640 Portugal launches a war of independence against Spain.

1642 19-year-old Blaise Pascal begins to develop the first practical mechanical calculator, the Pascaline, to help with the recording of taxes.

1642 Dutch sailor Abel Tasman discovers the island Van Diemen's Land (Tasmania) and becomes the first European to reach New Zealand.

1642 Galileo Galilei dies on 8th January. Isaac Newton is born on 25th December.

1642 Rembrandt paints *The Night Watch.*

1642 Isaac Aboab da Fonseca is appointed rabbi in Pernambuco, Brazil becoming the first rabbi of the Americas.

1642 Monteverdi composes *The Coronation of Poppea* one of the first operas to feature historical events and real people. It describes how Poppaea, mistress of Nero, achieves her ambition to be crowned empress.

1643 Evangelista Terricelli invents the barometer.

1644 The Ming Dynasty ends and the Qing dynasty begins – the last imperial dynasty of China, ruling until 1912 with a brief, abortive restoration in 1917.

1644 The *Basel problem* is posed by Pietro Mengoli and will puzzle mathematicians until solved by Leonhard Euler in 1731.

1645 *Theater of the World, or a New Atlas of Maps and Representations of All Regions,* edited by Willem and Joan Blaeu is printed.

1645 Wallpaper begins to replace tapestries as a wall decoration.

1646 Massachusetts enacts the death penalty for having a rebellious child.

1647 England's Puritan rulers ban Christmas. The following year they order that all playhouses and theatres are to be pulled down, all players seized and whipped, and anyone caught attending a play fined five shillings.

1648 The Russian explorer Semyon Dezhnyov reaches the area later named as the Bering Strait.

1648 Jan Baptista van Helmont introduces the word 'gas' (from the Greek word khaos) into the vocabulary.

1650 The first modern Palio horserace is held in Siena.

1650 Ann Greene, who had been hanged for infanticide in Edinburgh, wakes up on the autopsy table and is pardoned.

c1650 Diego Velázquez creates the *Portrait of Pope Innocent X.*

1650 The word 'obesity' is used for the first time in *Via Recta ad Vitam Longam* (Straight Road to Long Life) by Tobias Venner.

1650 *The Tenth Muse Lately Sprung Up in America* by Anne Bradstreet is the first volume of poetry to be published in the British North American colonies.

1650 Three-wheeled wheelchairs are invented in Nuremberg by watchmaker Stephen Farfler.

1651 Laws are passed in Massachusetts forbidding poor people from adopting excessive styles of dress.

1651 Thomas Hobbes book *Leviathan* establishes the foundation for most western political philosophy from the perspective of social contract theory.

c1651 Diego Velázquez paints the *Rokeby Venus* - the only surviving nude by this artist.

1652 George Fox forms The Religious Society of Friends (Quakers) with the philosophy: 'God does not dwell in temples or institutions made with hands, but freely in the hearts of men.'

1652 The Dutch establish the first European settlement in South Africa at Cape Town.

1652 The minuet comes into fashion at French court.

1654 Otto von Guericke demonstrates the force of atmospheric pressure using Magdeburg hemispheres before Ferdinand III, Holy Roman Emperor, and the Imperial Diet in Regensburg.

1654 Ferdinando II de' Medici sponsors the first weather-observing network with meteorological stations in Florence, Cutigliano, Vallombrosa, Bologna, Parma, Milan, Innsbruck, Osnabrück, Paris and Warsaw.

1654 Blaise Pascal lays the foundations of Probability Theory.

1655 *The Bibliotheca Thysiana* is erected, the only surviving 17th century example in the Netherlands of a building designed as a library.

1655 John Wallis introduces the symbol ∞ to represent infinity.

1656 The Black Madonna icon (Our Lady of Częstochowa) is crowned as Queen and Protector of Poland after a small force of monks from the Jasna Gora monastery fight off Swedish invaders and save their sacred icon.

1656 Diego Velázquez paints *Las Meninas* on which Picasso bases a series of 58 paintings over 300 years later.

1656 The Hospice de la Salpêtrière hospital in Paris is commissioned to replace a structure that had previously been used as a gunpowder factory, a prison and a holding place for the poor.

1656 Christiaan Huygens designs the first working pendulum clock.

1657 Stockholms Banco, the precursor to the central bank of Sweden, is founded and will become the first European bank to print banknotes four years later.

1657 The first eleven Quaker settlers arrive in New Amsterdam (later New York) and are allowed to practice their faith.

1657 Thomas Middleton's tragedy *Women Beware Women* is published posthumously.

1659 Parisian police raid a monastery and send the monks to prison for eating meat and drinking wine during Lent.

1659 Louis XIV meets his future wife, the Spanish Infanta, Maria Theresa at Isla de los Faisanes, a river island in the Basque country.

1660 The Alawite dynasty takes over in Morocco.

1660 Samuel Pepys has his first cup of tea, an event recorded in his diary.

1660 The first female actor appears on the stage as Desdemona in *Othello,* following the re-opening of the theatres in England.

1660 The great west window of Winchester Cathedral is reconstructed in a mosaic style using glass fragments dating from 1330 – an early prefiguring of collage art.

1662 Mr Punch of *Punch and Judy* makes his first recorded appearance.

1662 Boyle's Law describes the inverse relationship between volume and pressure of a gas at a constant temperature.

1662 A short-lived experiment with the first public buses holding 8 passengers begins in Paris.

1664 Kronenbourg lager is first produced.

1664 The palace and gardens at Versailles are commissioned by Louis XIV.

1665 Robert Hooke discovers that cork is made of 'tiny little rooms' which he calls 'cells'.

1665 Domenico Cassini, astronomy professor at Bologna University, refines the telescope and traces the meridian line in Patronio.

1665 Jan Vermeer paints *Girl with a Pearl Earring.*

1665 Margaret Porteous is the first person on record to die in the Great Plague of London.

1665 *The Royal Game of Chesse Play* by Gioacchino Greco, the first professional chess player, is published posthumously.

1665 Gabriël Metsu completes his painting *Lady Reading a Letter* the same year that Jan Vermeer paints *A Lady Writing a Letter.*

1666 Molière's comedy, *The Misanthrope,* premières at the Théâtre du Palais-Royal in Paris.

1666 Isaac Newton develops his *Method of Fluxions* (a version of calculus) during the Great Plague of London.

1667 Hook Head lighthouse in Co Wexford, Ireland is re-established. It is the oldest intact operational lighthouse in the world.

1667 Jean Baptiste Denys, physician to Louis XIV, performs the first human blood transfusion by transfusing the blood of a lamb to a 15-year old boy.

1667 The first use of the word 'Pandemonium' (the capital of Hell) appears in John Milton's *Paradise Lost*.

1667 French tapestry is established at the Gobelins Manufactory in Paris under the supervision of the royal painter, director and chief designer Charles Le Brun.

1669 Antonio Stradivari makes his first violin.

1669 The Chinese herbal medicine company Tongrentang is established in Beijing - now the largest producer of traditional Chinese medicine.

1669 Jan Swammerdam publishes *Historia Insectorum Generalis* in the Netherlands, explaining the process of metamorphosis in insects.

1670 The French colonize the island of Gorée near Dakar in modern Senegal.

1670 William Penn and William Mead are tried in London for preaching a Quaker sermon.

1671 The Académie royale d'architecture is founded by Louis XIV, the world's first school of architecture.

1671 The Observatoire de Paris – the world's first such national institution – is completed.

1672 Thomas Willis publishes the first English work on medical psychology, *Two Discourses concerning The Soul of Brutes, Which is that of the Vital and Sensitive of Man*.

1673 Leopold I, Spain, Netherlands and the Lutherans form an anti-French covenant.

1673 Antonio van Leewenhook uses powerful lenses to build microscopes and observes bee mouth parts and stings. Two years later he is the executor of Jan Vermeer's will.

1674 Father Jacques Marquette founds a mission on the shores of Lake Michigan to minister to the Illinois people. The mission will later grow into the city of Chicago.

1675 Construction of the Royal Greenwich Observatory begins.

1675 Gottfried Leibniz uses integral calculus for the first time to find the area under the graph of a function $y = f(x)$.

1675 The British Parliament orders the closure of all coffee houses as it is thought that they are centres of malicious gossip about the Government. The order is later reduced to a warning.

1675 A few days after the death of his beloved wife, the Japanese poet Saikaku composes a thousand-verse haikai poem over a period of about twelve hours.

1676 Ole Rømer makes the first quantitative measurements of the speed of light, showing that light has a finite speed and does not travel instantaneously.

1676 Antonie van Leeuwenhoek's credibility with the Royal Society is questioned when he sends a copy of his first observations of microscopic single-celled organisms.

1676 Part of a dinosaur bone is recovered from a limestone quarry. Robert Plot, who later becomes the first keeper of the Ashmolean Museum in Oxford, concludes that it is the thigh bone of a giant human.

1677 Jean Racine's tragedy *Phèdre* is first performed.

1677 *Ethics* by Benedict Spinoza is published posthumously - a work which opposes Descartes's mind–body dualism.

1678 Elena Piscopia becomes the first woman to be awarded a university degree (in philosophy) from the University of Padua.

1678 Robert Hooke publishes the Law of Elasticity including the solution to his Latin anagram on the concept *ceiiinosssttuv*, which translates as ut tensio, sic vis (as the extension, so the force).

1679 The *Habeas Corpus Act* is passed in England.

1679 Excavation begins on the Malpas Tunnel on the Canal du Midi in Hérault in France which will become Europe's first navigable canal tunnel.

c1680 The Byerley Turk thoroughbred horse is brought to England.

c1680 The Dodo (*Raphus cucullatus*), a flightless bird living on the island of Mauritius, becomes extinct.

1680 *La maison de Molière* is founded in Paris now known as *Comédie-Française*.

1680 Pueblo Indians capture Santa Fe (New Mexico) from the Spanish.

1681 A London woman is publicly flogged for the crime of 'involving herself in politics'.

1682 Louis XIV moves his court to Versailles.

1682 Japanese poet Saikaku writes the first of many novels *The Life of an Amorous Man*.

1682 Sophia Alekseyevna allies herself with a powerful courtier and politician, Prince Vasily Galitzine, and installs herself as regent of Russia during the minority of her brothers, Peter the Great and Ivan V.

1683 Wild boars are hunted to extinction in Britain.

1684 In England smuggled tea is drunk in far greater quantities than legally imported tea.

1684 James Chipperfield introduces performing animals at the Frost Fairs being held on the frozen River Thames in England.

1684 Gottfried Leibniz publishes the first account of differential calculus.

1685 Simon Ushakov paints *The Last Supper*.

1685 Fleeing from Jamaica after being charged with murder, Adam Baldridge founds a pirate base at Île Sainte-Marie in Madagascar.

1685 The revocation of the Edict of Nantes by Louis XIV forces 400,000 Hugenots to leave France.

1685 The first street lighting is introduced in London with oil lamps to be lit every tenth house on moonless winter nights.

1685 Charles Allen publishes the first book in English on dentistry, *The Operator for the Teeth*.

1685 Johann Sebastian Bach is born. George Frideric Handel is born.

1687 Isaac Newton describes universal gravitation and the three laws of motion in *Philosophiae Naturalis Principia Mathematica*.

1687 An Ottoman Turk ammunition dump inside the Parthenon is ignited by Venetian bombardment causing severe damage to the building and its sculptures.

1688 Edward Lloyd opens the London coffee house that becomes a popular meeting place for shipowners, merchants, insurance brokers and underwriters, later known as 'Lloyds of London'.

1689 The Tsar of Russia decrees the construction of the Great Siberian Route to China.

1690 John Locke's publication *Two Treatises of Government* argues for government by popular consent.

1690 The newspaper *Publick Occurrences Both Forreign & Domestick* is first published in Massachusetts after which it is suppressed by colonial authorities.

1690 Hishikawa Moronobu creates *Beauty looking back*, a ukiyo-e woodblock print.

1690 *The Court Midwife* by Justine Siegmund is published - the first German medical textbook written by a woman.

1690 Denis Papin builds a model of a piston steam engine, the first of its kind.

1690 The clarinet is invented in an evolution from an earlier instrument called the chalumeau, the first true single reed instrument.

1690 The Battle of the Boyne.

1690 Earliest recorded sighting of the planet Uranus by John Flamsteed, the first Astronomer Royal in England, who mistakenly catalogues it as the star 34 Tauri.

1691 Edmond Halley completes plans for a diving bell capable of remaining submerged for extended periods of time.

1692 The Salem witch trials begin in Salem Village, Massachusetts Bay Colony, with the charging of 3 women with witchcraft.

1693 China concentrates all its foreign trade in Canton forbidding European ships to land anywhere else.

1693 John Banks' historical play *The Innocent Usurper*, about Lady Jane Grey, is banned from the stage.

1694	The Bank of England is founded to act as the government's banker and debt-manager.
c1694	Johann Pachelbel composes *Canon in D*.
1695	Johann Sebastian Bach is orphaned and taken in by his cousin Johann Christoph Bach.
1695	English pirate Henry Every captures the Grand Mughal ship *Ganj-i-Sawai*, one of the most profitable raids in history. In response, Emperor Aurangzeb threatens to put an end to all English trading in India.
1695	A window tax is imposed in England and some windows are bricked up to avoid the tax. The same year a £2 fine is imposed for swearing.
1695	In Amsterdam, the bank Wed. Jean Deutz & Sn. floats the first sovereign bonds on the local market, issued for 12 years bearing 5% interest. The scheme is designed to fund a 1.5 million guilders loan to the Holy Roman Emperor.
1696	A famine wipes out almost a third of the population of Finland and a fifth of the population of Estonia.
1697	Antonio Stradivari makes the 'Castelbarco' cello and the following year the 'Cabriac' violin.
1697	The earliest known first-class cricket match takes place in Sussex.
1697	French writer Charles Perrault publishes a collection of then-popular fairy tales, including *Red Riding Hood* and *The Sleeping Beauty*.
1698	Tsar Peter I of Russia imposes a tax on beards: all men except priests and peasants are required to pay a tax of 100 rubles a year while commoners are required to pay one kopeck each.
1699	Isaac Newton is appointed as Master of the Mint.
1700	The death of Carlos II marks the end of the Hapsburg line in Spain.
1700	Russia begins numbering its calendar from the birth of Christ (Anno Domini) instead of since the Creation (Anno Mundi).
1700	William Penn, founder of the Province of Pennsylvania, begins monthly meetings advocating emancipation for black people.
1700	An inventory made for the Medici family of Florence includes the first documentary evidence for a piano, invented by their instrument keeper Bartolommeo Cristofori.
1701	The Empire of Ashanti in West Africa is founded when Osei Tutu is crowned as king.
1701	Jethro Tull invents a horse-drawn drill for sowing seeds in neat rows. His methods are adopted by many large landowners, and help form the basis of modern agriculture.
1701	Marsh's Library, the first public library in Ireland, is built.
1702	Guillaume Amontons is the first scientist to discuss the concept of an absolute zero of temperature.
1703	The Man in the Iron Mask dies in the Bastille.
1703	The ritual suicide by 47 Ronin (samurai) takes place after the assassination of Daimyo Kira Yoshinaka – an enemy of their former lord, Asano Naganori.
1704	Newton publishes *Opticks* describing how light can be split into a spectrum of different colours.
1705	The *Dublin Gazette* publishes its first edition with the strapline 'Published by Authority'.
1705	Edmond Halley notes that the comets seen in 1456, 1531, 1607 and 1682 were all the same comet and correctly predicts that it will return in 1758.
1705	The Venetian painter Rosalba Carriera becomes the first woman to be elected to the Accademia di San Luca in Rome.
1706	William Jones proposes using the symbol π to represent the ratio of the circumference of a circle to its diameter.
1706	Thomas Twining opens the first tea-room in Europe, located at 216 Strand, London.
1707	Mount Fuji begins to erupt in Japan.
1708	Calcareous hard-paste porcelain is produced for the first time in Europe at Dresden.
1709	Europe's coldest period in 500 years begins with parts of the Atlantic coast and the river Seine freezing – occurring during the time of low sun spot activity known as the Maunder Minimum.
1709	Alexander Selkirk is rescued from shipwreck on a desert island, inspiring the book Robinson Crusoe by Daniel Defoe.
1709	A collapsible umbrella is introduced in Paris.
1710	Jakob Christof Le Blon invents a three-colour printing process with red, blue, and yellow ink. He later adds black introducing the earliest four-colour printing process.
c1710	Antonio Vivaldi composes *Nulla in mundo pax sincera*.
1710	Alexis Littré is the first physician to suggest the possibility of performing a colostomy for obstruction of the colon.
1710	Beijing becomes the most populated city of the world, taking the lead from Constantinople (Istanbul).
1710	Ten ships leave London for the New York colony, carrying over 4,000 people.
1710	The world's first copyright legislation is introduced: Britain's *Statute of Anne*.
1711	The first Mardi Gras parade called Boeuf Gras (fatted ox) is held in Mobile, Alabama with 16 men pushing a large papier-mâché ox head on a cart.
1711	The 'calculus controversy' erupts - an argument between mathematicians Isaac Newton and Gottfried Leibniz over who had first invented calculus.
1712	A Newcomen steam engine is built to pump water out of mines in the Black Country of England, the first practical device to harness the power of steam to produce mechanical work.
1712	Arcangelo Corelli's *Concerti Grossi* are first performed.
1713	*Cato, a Tragedy* by Joseph Addison (with a prologue by Alexander Pope) is first performed.
1713	*Ars Conjectandi* (The Art of Conjecturing) by Jakob Bernoulli lays the foundation for probability theory.
1714	The British parliament votes to offer a reward 'for such person or persons as shall discover the Longitude.'
1714	Daniel Farenheit improves on Galileo's thermometer by sealing the mercury in glass.
1715	The first fire extinguisher is invented.
1716	A sculpture park is established in the Summer Garden (Letni Sad) at Saint Petersburg.
1716	America's first lighthouse, Boston Light, is built.
1716	The Kangxi Dictionary is published in China, laying the foundation for most references to Han characters studied today.
1717	Handel's *Water Music* premières on the river Thames based on a request from King George I. The concert is performed by 50 musicians playing on a barge near the royal barge from which the King listens with close friends.
1717	François-Marie Arouet is sentenced to imprisonment in the Bastille because of his satirical verse about the Regent of France. While there he writes his first literary work, *Œdipe*, using his adopted pen name, Voltaire.
1718	The Charitable Infirmary in Dublin is founded by six surgeons in Ireland and becomes the first public voluntary hospital in the British Isles.
1718	Blackbeard, the pirate, is killed in action at Ocracoke Inlet in North Carolina, after receiving five musketball wounds and twenty sword lacerations.
1719	The Principality of Liechtenstein is created within the Holy Roman Empire.
1719	*Robinson Crusoe* by Daniel Defoe is published.
1719	Prussia conducts the first systematic census in Europe.
1720	The Great Plague of Marseille is the last major outbreak of bubonic plague in Europe.
1720	J S Bach composes *Air on a G string*.
1720	The development of the post-chaise in France hugely increases the ease of travel overland and ushers in the era of 'The Grand Tour'.
1720	The first yacht club in the world, the Royal Cork Yacht Club, is founded in Ireland.
1722	The Safavids Persian dynasty ends. At the height of their power they controlled all of modern Iran, Azerbaijan and Armenia, most of Iraq, Georgia, Afghanistan and the Caucasus, as well as parts of Pakistan, Tajikistan and Turkey.

1722 At the age of 16 Benjamin Franklin adopts the pseudonym 'Mrs Silence Dogood', a middle-aged widow, in order to publish letters in *The New-England Courant*.

1722 Abraham de Moivre's formula connects complex numbers and trigonometry.

1723 Love suicides in Japan (Shinjū) reach their peak during the Edo period.

1723 Antonio Vivaldi composes The Four Seasons.

1724 Daniel Bernouilli expresses the numbers of the Fibonacci sequence in terms of the golden ratio.

1724 *Peter the Wild Boy*, a feral child, is found near Helpensen in Hanover, Germany.

1725 Navigator Vitus Bering is sent by Peter the Great to explore the North Pacific for potential colonization. The abundance of fur-bearing mammals on the Alaskan coast attracts Russian interest as overhunting has depleted Siberian stocks.

1725 The binary numeral system is invented by Basile Bouchon.

1725 The first meeting of a Masonic Grand Lodge of Ireland is held in Dublin.

1725 Catherine I becomes the first female Empress of Russia after the death of her husband Peter the Great. They had married secretly in 1707 and had twelve children, only two of whom survived into adulthood.

1726 Jonathan Swift writes *Gulliver's Travels*.

1727 An elderly woman known as Jenny Horne becomes the last alleged witch in the British Isles to be executed when she is burned at the stake in Dornoch, Scotland.

1727 Benjamin Franklin founds the *Junto*, a group of 'like minded aspiring artisans and tradesmen who hope to improve themselves while they improve their community.' From this group Franklin conceives the idea of a subscription library.

1727 Construction begins on the *Jantar Mantar* in Jaipur, a collection of architectural astronomical instruments commissioned by Maharaja Jai Singh II.

1727 Billiards becomes so popular that it is played in almost every café in Paris.

1727 Coffee plantations are established in Brazil.

1727 Euler uses the notation e in connection with the theory of natural logarithms, also known as Euler's number.

1729 The *Bayeux Tapestry* is re-discovered by scholars during its annual display in Bayeux Cathedral. Nearly 70 metres long, it depicts the events that led up to the Norman conquest of England culminating in the Battle of Hastings in 1066.

1730 *The Beggar's Opera* which lampoons the Italian opera style, is so popular that a deck of playing cards based on the characters is printed.

1731 Laura Bassi becomes the first official female university teacher on being appointed Professor of Anatomy at the University of Bologna at the age of 21.

1731 Marie Angelique, a feral child (later known as The Maid of Châlons) is discovered in Songy in Champagne, France.

1731 The orrery is invented as an apparatus to show the relative positions of heavenly bodies in the solar system by using balls moved by wheelwork.

1731 Johann Scheuchzer's *Physica Sacra*, which attempts to provide a scientific explanation of Biblical history, is published.

1732 Canaletto paints *View of the Entrance to the Arsenale di Venezia*.

1732 Philip Miller of the Chelsea Physic Garden sends cotton seeds to Georgia, America.

1733 The flying shuttle loom is patented, enabling faster weaving and increasing demand for yarn.

1733 The perambulator is invented by architect William Kent for the children of the 3rd Duke of Devonshire.

1733 De Moivre publishes work on the normal curve as an approximation of the Binomial distribution.

1735 The first successful appendectomy is performed by French surgeon Claudius Aymand in London.

1735 John Harrison invents the first of his marine chronometers, which enables sailors to calculate their longitude with accuracy.

1735 Charles Marie de La Condamine leads an expedition of French scientists to Peru to try to calculate the circumference of the earth.

1735 Leonhard Euler solves the problem of the seven bridges of Königsberg, laying down the foundations of graph theory and prefiguring the concept of topology.

1735 Carl Linnaeus publishes his classification system *Systema Naturae*. The philosopher Rousseau sends him the message, 'tell him I know no greater man on earth.'

1737 The oldest existing English language daily newspaper in the world, *The Belfast News Letter*, is founded in Ireland.

1737 *Il Newtonianismo per le Dame* by Francesco Algarotti is published. A translation by Elizabeth Carter is published two years later under the title *Sir Isaac Newton's Philosophy Explain'd for the Use of the Ladies*.

1738 Franz Ketterer invents the cuckoo clock.

1738 A collection of essays, *Propositiones Philosophicae* by the mathematician Maria Gaetana Agnesi is published. Many of the essays include her conviction that women should be educated.

1738 Bernoulli's principle is published in *Hydrodynamica*.

1740 Anna Ivanovna, Empress of Russia, arranges a marriage for Prince Galitzine who has displeased her. She forces him to spend his wedding night with his bride in an elaborate ice palace, complete with ice bed, ice furniture and ice sculptures.

1740 Charles VI, Holy Roman Emperor dies after consuming death cap mushrooms.

1740 The reign of Frederick the Great, Frederick II King of Prussia begins.

1741 The Maria Theresa thaler, a silver bullion coin still used in world trade, is first minted.

1741 Vitus Bering and Aleksei Chirikiv are the first Europeans to land in southern Alaska.

1742 Handel's *Messiah* is performed for the first time before an audience of approximately 700 people in a Music Hall in Fishamble Street, Dublin, Ireland.

1742 The Goldbach conjecture is proposed: every even number greater than 2 is the sum of two primes.

1743 Natalia Lopukhina is flogged in front of the Twelve Collegia building in Saint Petersburg for her alleged conspiracy at the Russian court.

1744 The Great Comet is visible until April, one of the brightest comets ever seen (C/1743 X1).

1744 Engravings of Susanna Drury's illustrations of the Giant's Causeway in Antrim brings the rock formation of polygonal columns to wide European notice.

1744 The first recorded women's cricket match takes place in England.

1745 William Hogarth completes his series of six satirical paintings *Marriage à la Mode: The Marriage Settlement, The Tête à Tête, The Inspection, the Toilette, The Bagnio and The Lady's Death*.

1745 The Company of Surgeons separates from the Company of Barbers of London.

1745 Pieter van Musschenbroek invents the Leyden jar, a device for storing electric charge - the first capacitor.

1746 The Dress Act comes into force making the wearing of 'the Highland Dress', including tartan or a kilt, illegal in Scotland.

1747 A tribal council of native Pashtun people creates modern Afghanistan and Ahmad Shah Durrani becomes King.

1747 In one of the first controlled trials, James Lind shows that the eating of citrus fruits prevents scurvy.

1748 Eva Ekeblad becomes the first female member of the Royal Swedish Academy of Sciences.

1748 The first comprehensive excavation of Pompeii begins.

1748 Lewis Paul invents a machine for carding - a mechanical process that separates fibres and assembles them into a loose strand suitable for spinning and weaving.

1748 The Kabuki drama Chushingura, based on the revenge suicide by 47 Ronin (samurai) is performed.

1748 Montesquieu advocates the separation of powers in *The Spirit of the Laws.*

1749 The first official performance of George Frideric Handel's *Music for the Royal Fireworks* finishes early due to the outbreak of fire.

1749 Denis Diderot writes *Lettre sur les aveugles à l'usage de ceux qui voient* (Letter on the Blind For the Use of Those Who See). The subject is a discussion of the interrelation between man's reason and the knowledge acquired through perception of the five senses.

1750 Riots break out in Paris, fuelled by rumours of police abducting children.

1750 Hannah Snell, a British woman who had disguised herself as a man to become a soldier, reveals her sex to her Royal Marines compatriots.

1750 Galley slavery is abolished in Europe.

1751 Robert Whytt discovers the nature of the pupillary reflex, the contraction of the pupil in response to light, later known as Whytt's reflex.

1752 The *Khan As'ad Pasha* in Damascus is completed.

1752 The *Tiergarten Schönbrunn* is established in Vienna - the world's oldest zoo.

1752 The world's first steeplechase is held as the result of a wager between Cornelius O'Callaghan and Edmund Blake who race four miles cross-country from Buttevant Church to St. Leger Church in Doneraile, Cork, Ireland.

1752 The Gregorian calendar is adopted by England and its colonies 170 years after the first countries made the changeover.

1752 Benjamin Franklin flies a kite during a thunderstorm and demonstrates that lightning is an electrical discharge.

1753 Old Blush, a China rose derived from *Rosa chinensis,* is the first East Asian rose to reach Europe.

1754 *Discourse on the Origin and Basis of Inequality Among Men* is written by philosopher Jean-Jacques Rousseau in response to an essay competition: *What is the origin of inequality among men, and is it authorized by natural law?*

1755 Franz Joseph Haydn composes his first string quartet.

c1755 Joseph Black discovers 'fixed air', now known as carbon dioxide.

1755 Leopold Mozart composes *Divertimento in F major 'Musical Sleigh Ride'.*

1756 St Patrick's Day is celebrated in New York City for the first time, at the Crown and Thistle Tavern.

1756 The Marine Society is founded in London, the world's oldest seafarers' charity.

1756 François Boucher paints portraits of Madame de Pompadour.

1757 *A Philosophical Enquiry into the Origin of Our Ideas of the Sublime and Beautiful* by Edmund Burke is published.

1759 Emilie du Châtelet's translation and commentary on Newton's *Principia Mathematica* is published posthumously. Voltaire, one of her lovers, declared in a letter to his friend, King Frederick II of Prussia, that du Châtelet was 'a great man whose only fault was being a woman'.

1759 The Royal Botanic Gardens at Kew in London are founded.

1760 Dr James Fordyce's two-volume compendium *Sermons for Young Women* is published.

1760 Western countries pay 3,000,000 ounces of silver for Chinese goods.

1761 Johann Heinrich Lambert proves that π is irrational.

1761 The theory of latent heat proposed by Joseph Black marks the beginning of thermodynamics.

1761 Astronomers from Britain, France, Sweden and Russia set up telescopes across the globe to time the transit of Venus across the Sun and thus calculate the distance between the Earth and the Sun.

1761 The first veterinary school in the world is created in Lyon by equerry Claude Bourgelat.

1762 Kobayashi Issa is born. He becomes one of the four great haiku masters with Bashō (b1644), Buson (b1716) and Shiki (b1867).

1762 The Society for Equitable Assurances on Lives and Survivorships is established in London, pioneering mutual insurance using actuarial science.

1762 The Trevi Fountain in Rome is completed after thirty years.

1762 Construction starts on the Petit Trianon, a small château at Versailles, commissioned by Louis XV for his mistress, Madame de Pompadour.

1762 Rousseau's concept of the 'noble savage' appears in his publication *Of The Social Contract, Or Principles of Political Right.*

1764 The spinning jenny, a multi-spool spinning wheel, is invented by James Hargreaves.

1764 Cesare Beccaria writes *On Crime and Punishment,* a work which includes the condemnation of torture and the death penalty.

1764 The first state-financed higher education institution for women in Europe is ordered by decree under Catherine the Great, Empress of Russia.

1765 Sturm und Drang (Storm and Urge) begins - a free expression movement in German literature and music.

1765 James Watt makes a breakthrough in the development of the steam engine by constructing a model with a separate condenser.

1766 Henry Cavendish discovers hydrogen which he calls 'inflammable air' noted in his paper *On Factitious Airs.* Antoine Lavoisier later reproduces Cavendish's experiment and gives the element its name.

1767 *The Nautical Almanac* published by the Royal Greenwich Observatory gives mariners the means to find their longitude while at sea using tables of lunar distances.

1767 John Spilsbury makes the first jigsaw puzzle. He intends to teach geography by cutting maps into pieces but soon jigsaws are made for entertainment.

1768 Bougainvillea is first classified in Brazil by Philibert Commerçon.

1768 Joseph Wright of Derby paints *An Experiment on a Bird in the Air Pump.* The painting depicts a natural philosopher recreating one of Robert Boyle's air pump experiments, in which a bird is deprived of air, before a group of onlookers.

1768 *Si Dieu n'existait pas, il faudrait l'inventer* (If God did not exist, it would be necessary to invent him), Voltaire.

1768 Corsica is sold to France by the Republic of Genoa. Napoleon Bonaparte is born on the island the following year.

1769 Captain Cook observes the Transit of Venus from Tahiti at a location still known as Point Venus.

1770 Captain Cook and the crew of the *Endeavour* land in Botany Bay.

1771 Luigi Boccherini composes *String Quintet in E.*

1771 Jean-Baptiste-Siméon Chardin paints *Autoportrait aux Besicles.*

1772 *The Art of War,* a Chinese military treatise written during the Warring States period (476BC – 221BC), is translated into French by the Jesuit Jean Joseph Marie Amiot.

1772 The partition of Poland marks the end of the Polish–Lithuanian Commonwealth.

1773 The East India Company starts operations in Bengal to smuggle opium into China.

1773 John Harrison receives the Longitude prize for his invention of the first marine chronometer.

1773 In protest against the tax policy of the British government, colonists board ships in Boston harbour and throw the cargo of tea into the sea - The Boston Tea Party.

1774 Empress Maria Theresa of Austria develops the first state education system, The General School for Boys.

1774 Joseph Priestley isolates oxygen in the form of a gas which he calls 'dephlogisticated air'.

1775 The American Revolution.

1775 On his second voyage, Captain Cook uses a marine chronometer (a copy of John Harrison's H4 clock) to measure longitude. *Resolution* is the first ship known to cross the Antarctic Circle.

1775 Catherine the Great gives the nobles absolute control over their serfs.

1776 In his publication, *The Wealth of Nations,* Adam Smith warns of the 'collusive nature of business interests, which may form cabals or monopolies, fixing the highest price which can be squeezed out of the buyers'.

1776 United States Declaration of Independence.

1776 The Bavarian Illuminati is founded by Adam Weishaupt with an initial membership of five.

1777 Morocco becomes the first nation to formally recognize the American colonies.

1777 The Code Duello is adopted by the gentlemen of counties Tipperary, Galway, Mayo, Sligo and Roscommon in Ireland as 'the form' for pistol duels. It becomes widely adopted throughout the English-speaking world.

c1777 Francisco Goya paints *The Parasol*.

1778 The term 'thoroughbred' is first used in the United States in an advertisement in a Kentucky gazette to describe a New Jersey stallion called Pilgarlick.

1778 The Tây Sơn Dynasty is established in Vietnam.

1779 An iron bridge is erected across the River Severn in England, the world's first bridge built entirely of cast iron.

1781 *Critique of Pure Reason* by Immanuel Kant is published.

1781 French spy François Henri de la Motte is hanged and drawn before a large crowd at Tyburn in London for high treason.

1781 The world's first Bagpipe competition is held at the Masonic Arms, Falkirk, Scotland.

1781 Charles Messier publishes the final catalogue of Messier objects. All of the Messier objects are visible with binoculars or small telescopes (under favourable conditions).

1782 In Switzerland, Anna Göldi is the last person in the world to be legally sentenced to death for witchcraft.

1782 The bald eagle is chosen as the emblem of the United States of America.

1782 The largest literary compilation in China's history, the Siku Quanshu is completed, surpassing the Yongle Encyclopedia of the 15th century. The books are bound in 36,381 volumes, comprising 2.3 million pages and approximately 800 million Chinese characters.

1783 The first manned hot-air balloon, designed by the Montgolfier brothers, takes off from the Bois de Boulogne.

1783 Ireland's last grey wolf is killed.

1784 Explorer Grigory Shelekhov founds Russia's first permanent settlement in Alaska at Three Saints Bay.

c1784 Queen Marie Antoinette is implicated in participating in a crime to defraud the crown jewellers of the cost of a diamond necklace.

1785 A hot air balloon crashes in Tullamore, Ireland, causing a fire that burns down about 100 houses, making it the world's first aviation disaster.

1785 Friedrich Schiller writes *Ode to Joy*, a poem on which the closing choral section of Beethoven's *Ninth Symphony* (1824) is based.

1786 Tuscany is the first European state to abolish the death penalty.

1787 Antonio Canova's statue *Psyche Revived by Cupid's Kiss* is commissioned.

1787 HMS Bounty sets sail for the South Seas under Captain William Bligh.

1787 Mozart's *Don Giovanni* is first performed in the Estates Theatre in Prague.

1789 Aboriginal Woollarawarre Bennelong is kidnapped and brought to the settlement at Sydney Cove to act as interlocutor between the British and the Eora people.

1789 George Washington is elected as the first President of the United States.

1789 Giacomo Casanova starts writing *Histoire de ma vie (Story of my Life)*.

1789 Storming of the Bastille, 14th July. The prison contains just seven inmates at the time of its storming.

1789 Jeremy Bentham, the founder of modern utilitarianism, argues that 'all punishment in itself is evil; it ought only to be admitted in as far as it promises to exclude some greater evil.' John Stuart Mill will later become Bentham's student.

1789 The Bill of Rights: the first ten amendments to the American constitution.

1791 Giovanni Battista Guglielmini demonstrates the rotation of the Earth in Bologna.

1791 Wolfgang Amadeus Mozart composes *The Magic Flute* and the *Clarinet Concerto*. He dies at the age of 35 leaving the unfinished *Requiem in D Minor*, his 626th composition.

1791 Olympe de Gouges publishes Déclaration des droits de la femme et de la citoyenne, *Declaration of the Rights of Woman and the Female Citizen*.

1791 Luigi Galvani publishes his discoveries in animal electricity, later known as Galvanism.

1791 Toussaint Breda (Louverture) leads a slave rebellion in the French colony of Saint Domingue on Hispaniola.

1792 Mary Wollstonecraft writes *A Vindication of the Rights of Woman*. Her daughter, born five years later, is Mary Shelley, author of *Frankenstein*.

1792 The city of Freetown in Sierra Leone is founded by abolitionist John Clarkson as a land for freed African American slaves.

1793 Jacques-Louis David paints *La Mort de Marat*.

1794 Erasmus Darwin, grandfather of Charles Darwin, publishes *Zoonomia*, a medical work including arguments that all extant organisms are descended from one common ancestor.

1794 The French revolutionary government under the leadership of Maximilien Robespierre votes for the abolition of slavery.

1795 The British Royal Navy makes the use of lemon juice mandatory to prevent scurvy.

1796 Edward Jenner discovers that immunity to smallpox can be produced by inoculation with material from the cowpox virus, a process that will become known as vaccination.

1796 Jean Senebier demonstrates that green plants consume carbon dioxide and release oxygen under the influence of light.

c1796 Roulette (little wheel) is first played in Paris.

1797 Joseph Haydn composes *Gott erhalte Franz den Kaiser* as an anthem for the birthday of the Austrian Emperor Francis II. The melody will later be used for the German national anthem.

1797 The XYZ Affair is caused by an international incident in which the French Foreign Minister, Talleyrand, demands bribes and a loan in exchange for facilitating diplomatic negotiations between France and the United States.

1797 Horatio Nelson is wounded at the Battle of Santa Cruz and loses his arm.

1797 London haberdasher John Hetherington wears a top hat in public causing a near riot and is arrested for a breach of the peace.

1798 Samuel Taylor Coleridge writes *The Rime of the Ancyent Marinere*.

1799 Jeanne Geneviève Labrosse becomes the first woman to jump from a balloon with a parachute, from an altitude of 900 meters.

1799 A 12-year-old boy, Conrad Reed, finds what he describes as a 'heavy yellow rock' in Cabarrus County, North Carolina and makes it a doorstop in his home. The rock is discovered to be gold in 1802, initiating the first gold rush in the United States.

1799 Lithography is invented by the Austrian printer Alois Senefelder by using a matrix of fine-grained limestone.

1799 The Rosetta Stone, an ancient Egyptian stele inscribed with a decree issued at Memphis in 196 BC for King Ptolemy V, is discovered near the town of Rashid in the Nile Delta.

1800 As the result of a professional disagreement over the 'galvanic response' advocated by Galvani, Alessandro Volta invents the voltaic pile, an early electric battery which produces a steady electric current.

1800 The Dutch East India Company goes bankrupt. The islands of Indonesia are known as the Dutch East Indies until Indonesia's independence 149 years later.

1801 The first asteroid is discovered and named Ceres.

1801 Elgin's agents start to remove many of the surviving sculptures from the Parthenon, Propylaea and Erechtheum.

1801 Ultraviolet radiation is discovered by Johann Wilhelm Ritter.

1803 Irish rebel Robert Emmet makes a speech from the dock, on the eve of his execution for high treason, with the closing words, 'When my country takes her place among the nations of the earth, then and not till then, let my epitaph be written. I have done.'

1803 John Dalton begins using symbols to represent different elements and publishes *Atomic Theory of the Elements* the following year.

1803 Thomas Young's double slit experiment demonstrates the wave form of light.

1804 Haiti gains independence from France and becomes the first black republic as a result of the successful slave revolt.

1804 Alexander Hamilton, one of the founding fathers of America, is shot during a duel with Vice President Aaron Burr and dies the next day.

1805 Mohammad Ali Pasha becomes the self-declared Khedive (Governor) of Egypt and Sudan.

1805 The Battle of Trafalgar.

1805 *Conversations on Chemistry* by Jane Marcet is published anonymously. It becomes one of the first elementary science textbooks and provides inspiration for the young Michael Faraday.

1805 The Horse Patrol, a mounted law enforcement force, is founded in London.

1806 The abdication of Francis II brings the Holy Roman Empire to an end after almost a millennium.

1807 The *Clermont* leaves New York City for Albany on the Hudson River, inaugurating the first commercial steamboat service in the world.

1807 The world's oldest international football stadium, the Racecourse Ground, opens in Wales, although it will not host football games until 1872.

1807 Pall Mall in London is the first street to be lit by gas.

1808 In Vienna Ludwig van Beethoven conducts the première of his *Fifth Symphony, Sixth Symphony, Fourth Piano Concerto* and *Choral Fantasy.*

1808 Johann Wolfgang von Goethe publishes *Faust.*

1808 The *Smolny Institute for Noble Maidens* is established in St Petersburg - the first state-financed higher education institution for women in Europe.

1809 The wearing of masks at balls is forbidden in Boston, Massachusetts.

1809 Charles Darwin and Abraham Lincoln are both born on 12th February.

1810 A pioneering study of the localization of mental functions in the brain is published popularizing the study of phrenology.

1810 The marriage of Napoleon and Josephine is annulled and Napoleon marries Marie-Louise of Austria.

1810 Bernardo O'Higgins Riquelme joins the revolt against the French-dominated Spanish government in Chile. He is later known as one of the founding fathers of Chile.

1812 Lord Byron publicly defends the Luddites, a group of English textile artisans who violently protest against their replacement with unskilled workers and machinery.

1812 Grimms' Fairy Tales is first published under the title *Kinder und Hausmärchen* (Children's and Household Tales).

1812 Laplace's Demon - an essay on a deterministic world – is published: 'Given the precise location and momentum of every atom in the universe then past and future values for any given time can be calculated from the laws of classical mechanics.'

1813 *Pride and Prejudice* by Jane Austen is published.

1814 Missionaries in New Zealand make the first attempts to write down the Māori language.

1815 A meteorite ejected 11 million years previously from Mars falls in Chassigny, Haute-Marne, France.

1815 Giovanni Belzoni, formerly a strongman at fairs, removes the colossal bust of Ramesses II, the Young Memnon, from the Ramesseum at Thebes.

1815 The metronome is invented by Johann Maelzel.

1815 Humphry Davy invents the Davy lamp allowing miners to work safely in the presence of flammable gases.

1815 Napoleon is exiled on the island of St Helena after defeat at the Battle of Waterloo.

1816 The stethoscope is invented by René Laennec.

1818 *Frankenstein; or, The Modern Prometheus* by Mary Shelley is published.

1818 *Ozymandias* by Percy Bysshe Shelley is published.

1819 The Prado museum in Madrid is completed.

1820 Antarctica is sighted for the first time by Imperial Russian Navy captain Fabian Gottlieb von Bellingshausen during his circumnavigation of the globe.

1820 Hans Christian Ørsted discovers the relationship between electricity and magnetism.

1820 The *Venus de Milo* statue is discovered on the Greek island of Milos.

1820 The Cato Street Conspiracy, a plot to murder all British cabinet ministers, is discovered.

1820 Spain sells part of Florida to the US for $5,000,000.

1821 The Santa Fe Trail is established and becomes the first international trade route between the United States and Mexico. Americans routinely trade with the Comanche along the trail.

1821 Michael Faraday demonstrates the conversion of electrical energy into mechanical energy by means of electromagnetism, paving the way for the development of the electric motor.

1821 The first commercially successful chronograph is invented for King Louis XVIII who enjoyed watching horse races, but wanted to know exactly how long each race lasted.

1822 The hieroglyphs on the Rosetta Stone are deciphered using the fact that the information appears in three scripts: Ancient Egyptian hieroglyphs, Demotic script and Ancient Greek.

1822 The last public whipping is carried out in Edinburgh.

1822 A group of freed slaves from the United States arrive in West Africa and found Monrovia (Liberia).

1823 Charles Babbage is awarded £1700 to develop his design for the Difference Engine.

1823 *The Red Lady of Paviland,* an Upper Paleolithic-era human male skeleton 33,000 years old dyed in red ochre, is found in limestone caves in south Wales.

1823 Eleven-year-old Franz Liszt gives a concert after which he is congratulated by Ludwig van Beethoven.

1823 The Mexican Empire dissolves: Costa Rica joins El Salvador, Guatemala, Honduras and Nicaragua as the United Provinces of Central America.

1823 Olbers' paradox is first described. Also called the dark night sky paradox, it explains that the darkness of the night sky conflicts with the assumption of an infinite and eternal static universe.

1824 John Dickens (father of Charles Dickens) is imprisoned in Marshalsea Debtors' Prison for a debt of £40 and 10 shillings that he owes a baker.

1825 Minh Mang outlaws the teaching of Christianity in Vietnam.

1825 Food canning is patented.

1825 Construction begins on the Thames Tunnel, the first tunnel built underneath a navigable river.

1826 *The Last of the Mohicans: A Narrative of 1757* by James Fenimore Cooper is published.

1827 *Freedom's Journal,* the first African-American owned and published newspaper in the United States, is founded in New York City by John Russwurm.

1827 The paddle steamer *Curaçao* makes the first transatlantic crossing by steam, from Hellevoetsluis in the Netherlands to Paramaribo in Suriname.

1827 A giraffe is sent as a gift from Mehmet Ali Pasha, Viceroy of Egypt, to King Charles X of France. It walks from Marseilles to Paris becoming one of the first giraffes to be seen in Europe for over three centuries.

1827 John Walker invents the first friction match naming it the Lucifer.

1828 Ányos Jedlik is the first person to build and demonstrate a practical DC motor containing the essential components of a stator, rotor and commutator.

1829 The Swan River Colony (later to become the cities of Perth and Fremantle) is founded in Western Australia. This secures the western third of the Australian landmass for the British.

1829 Oxford and Cambridge universities compete in the first university boat race, held at Henley, UK.

1829 The patent for an instrument called the accordion is applied for by Cyrill Demian in Vienna.

1830 Hector Berlioz's *Symphonie Fantastique,* has its world premiere in Paris.

1830 *The Book of Mormon* by Joseph Smith is published.

1831 The French Foreign Legion is founded.

1831 Katsushika Hokusai creates the woodblock print series *Thirty-six Views of Mount Fuji.*

1831 *The Hunchback of Notre-Dame* by Victor Hugo is published.

1831 Robert Brown identifies the cell nucleus.

1831 The Royal Zoological Society of Dublin is founded by members of the medical profession who wish to study both living and dead animals.

1833 The first semi-conductor effect is recorded by Michael Faraday.

1833 Alexandr Pushkin writes the poem *The Bronze Horseman: A Petersburg Tale.*

1834 The Spanish Inquisition, which began in the 15th century, is suppressed by royal decree.

1834 Eugène Delacroix paints *The Women of Algiers.*

1835 Charles Darwin reaches the Galapagos archipelago aboard the *HMS Beagle.*

1835 Hans Christian Andersen's *Fairy Tales Told for Children* is published.

1835 The *New York Sun* prints the first of six instalments of the 'Great Moon Hoax'.

1836 The first printed literature in Assyrian Neo-Aramaic is produced by American missionary Justin Perkins.

1836 Samuel Colt patents the first revolving barrel multi-shot firearm.

1837 The Berlin Foundry Cup (5th century BC) is acquired for the Antikensammlung in Berlin, Germany.

1838 In the U.S. the people of the Cherokee Nation are forcibly relocated – the Trail of Tears.

1838 The paddle steamer *SS Sirius* makes the transatlantic crossing from Cork in Ireland to New York in eighteen days - the first holder of the *Blue Riband* award.

1838 Proteins are named by Jöns Jakob Berzelius.

1838 Richard Lamin proposes the concept of an 'indivisible quantity of electric charge' to explain the chemical properties of atoms. These will later be named electrons.

1839 The first photograph of the Moon is taken by Louis Daguerre.

1839 Charles Goodyear develops a process to vulcanize rubber.

1840 The Penny Black, the world's first postage stamp, is issued.

1840 Samuel Morse is granted a patent for his invention of the telegraph.

1840 The Māori sign the Treaty of Waitangi, giving control to the British in exchange for protection and guaranteed Māori possession of their lands.

1841 John Rand patents the first collapsible metal tube for artist's oil paint replacing breakable glass vials and leaky animal bladders. Renoir later observes 'without paint in tubes, there would be no impressionism.'

1841 Charles Mackay publishes *Extraordinary Popular Delusions and the Madness of Crowds.*

1841 China cedes Hong Kong to Great Britain.

1843 William Rowan Hamilton writes the fundamental formula for quaternions on Broome Bridge in Dublin, Ireland $i^2 = j^2 = k^2 = ijk = -1$.

1843 Joule studies the nature of heat, leading to the theory of the conservation of energy.

1844 The Great Auk becomes extinct.

1845 William Parsons, 3rd Earl of Rosse, builds the Leviathan of Parsonstown, a 72-inch reflecting telescope at Birr Castle in Ireland. It remains the world's largest telescope until the early 20th century.

1845 Frederick Douglass publishes his autobiography *Narrative of the Life of Frederick Douglass, an American Slave.*

1845 The first law relating to rugby boots is formulated: no player may wear projecting nails or iron plates on the heels or soles of his shoes or boots.

1846 The Oregon Treaty establishes the 49th parallel from the Rocky Mountains to the Strait of Juan de Fuca as the border between the United States and Canada.

1846 The anaesthetic properties of chloroform are discovered and used on an obstetric patient for the first time.

1846 The Great Famine begins in Ireland when three quarters of the potato crop is lost to blight *Phytophthora Infestans.*

1846 Emily Brontë publishes *Wuthering Heights* under the pen name of Ellis Bell. The following year *Jane Eyre* by Charlotte Brontë is published under the pen name of Currer Bell.

1848 The California Gold Rush is prompted when James Marshall finds flakes of gold at Sutter's Mill, in Coloma.

1848 Dante Gabriel Rossetti founds the Pre-Raphaelite Brotherhood with William Holman Hunt and John Everett Millais.

1848 Kelvin establishes an absolute scale of temperature.

1848 The campaign for women's suffrage in the US begins at the Seneca Falls Convention. The following year Elizabeth Blackwell becomes the world's first openly identified woman to graduate from a medical school.

1849 Fyodor Dostoyevsky serves four years of exile with hard labour at a Katorga prison camp in Omsk, Siberia.

1849 Fizeau's rotating wheel becomes the first terrestrial method used for measuring the velocity of light.

1850 The Tara Brooch (700 AD) is found in County Meath, Ireland.

1850 Rudolf Clausius proposes the basic principles of the Second Law of Thermodynamics.

1851 Foucault's Pendulum, a 28kg brass-coated lead bob on a 67m long wire, is suspended from the dome of the Pantheon in Paris.

1851 John Everett Millais paints *Ophelia.*

1851 *Moby-Dick* by Herman Melville is published.

1851 The Great Exhibition is held at the Crystal Palace in London.

1851 The first modern chess tournament is won by Adolf Anderssen.

1851 Victor Hugo uses the phrase 'United States of Europe' in a speech to the French National Assembly.

1854 George Boole develops Boolean algebra based on the mathematical analysis of logic.

1854 Florence Nightingale leaves for the Crimea with 38 other nurses.

1855 Safety Matches using red phosphorus on the striking surface are introduced.

1855 Alexander II, later known as Alexander the Liberator for freeing the serfs, becomes Emperor of Russia. His reign ends in 1881 when he is killed in a fourth assassination attempt.

1855 David Livingstone discovers and names Victoria Falls - also known as Mosi-oa-Tunya (the smoke that thunders) - on the Zambezi river.

1856 Gustave Flaubert's *Madame Bovary* is published. Flaubert is accused of obscenity by public prosecutors and put on trial the following year.

1858 Felix Mendelssohn's *Wedding March* is played at the marriage of Queen Victoria's daughter Victoria to Crown Prince Frederick of Prussia.

1858 *Gray's Anatomy* is published.

1858 Möbius and Listing introduce the Möbius strip.

1858 The first transatlantic telegraph cable is laid across the floor of the Atlantic from Valentia Island in Ireland to Heart's Content in eastern Newfoundland. The communication time between North America and Europe is reduced from ten days to minutes.

1859 Building begins on the Suez Canal in Egypt.

1859 Big Ben is completed.

1859 *On the Origin of Species* by Charles Darwin is published.

1859 *The Rubáiyát of Omar Khayyám* is published - Edward FitzGerald's translation of a selection of poems written by the 12th century Persian poet, mathematician and astronomer.

1860 Bunsen and Kirchhoff develop analytical spectroscopy.

1860 Construction begins on the London Underground.

1860 Florence Nightingale opens the first non-religious nursing school in the world.

1861 Auguste Mariette begins the excavation of the Temple of Edfu from the sands on the west bank of the Nile.

1861 James Clerk Maxwell's equations demonstrate that electricity, magnetism and light are all manifestations of the same phenomenon, namely the electromagnetic field.

1861 *Silas Marner* by George Eliot (Mary Ann Evans) is published.

1862 Louis Pasteur develops a process in which liquids such as milk are heated to kill most bacteria and moulds already present within them – later known as pasteurization.

1863 The Gettysburg Address by President Abraham Lincoln.

1864 Frederic William Burton paints *Hellelil and Hildebrand* known in English as *Meeting on the Turret Stairs*.

1864 The Thirteenth Amendment to the United States Constitution outlaws slavery and involuntary servitude, except as punishment for a crime.

1865 Rev Rasmus Malling-Hansen of Denmark invents the Hansen Writing Ball, the first commercially sold typewriter.

1865 Rudolf Clausius introduces the concept of entropy.

1865 Gregor Mendel founds the new science of genetics, based on his cultivation and testing of some 29,000 pea plants.

1865 *Tristan und Isolde* by Richard Wagner premières in Munich.

1867 Colonies now known as Nova Scotia, New Brunswick, Ontario and Quebec join to create the Dominion of Canada.

1867 *Das Kapital* by Karl Marx is published.

1867 The United States accepts the Russian Emperor Alexander II's offer to sell Alaska for $7.2 million.

1867 The Marquess of Queensberry rules for boxing are published.

1868 *Little Women* by Louisa May Alcott is published.

1869 Dmitri Mendeleev creates the periodic table of elements.

1869 The Suez Canal opens, connecting the Mediterranean with the Red Sea.

1869 John Tyndall demonstrates and explains the Tyndall effect - why the sky is blue and the sunset is red.

1869 *War and Peace* by Leo Tolstoy is published.

1869 Édouard Manet creates the series of paintings titled *The Execution of Emperor Maximilian* depicting the execution by firing squad of Emperor Maximilian I of the short-lived, second Mexican Empire.

1870 Louis Pasteur and Robert Koch establish the germ theory of disease.

1871 Publication of *The Descent of Man and Selection in Relation to Sex* by Charles Darwin includes his first formal use of the term evolution.

1871 The first rugby union international game results in a 4–1 win by Scotland over England.

1871 *Aida* by Giuseppe Verdi is first performed at the Khedivial Opera House in Cairo.

1872 Claude Monet paints *Impression, Sunrise*.

1872 Yellowstone National Park is established as the first National Park in the world.

1872 The science of oceanography is born when the HMS Challenger expedition departs from Portsmouth with five scientists and one artist aboard – they will discover 4,700 previously unknown species.

1873 Charles Hermite proves that the mathematical constant e is a transcendental number.

1873 *Anna Karenina* by Leo Tolstoy is published in serial instalments in the periodical *The Russian Messenger*.

1874 The New York Zoo hoax - a New York Herald article warns that dangerous animals from Central Park Zoo are loose in the city causing widespread panic despite the article ending with the words 'the entire story given above is a pure fabrication.'

1874 Edvard Grieg starts composing the incidental music for Ibsen's play *Peer Gynt*.

1875 The first organized indoor game of ice hockey is played at the Victoria Skating Rink in Montreal, Canada.

1875 The Metre Convention is signed in Paris.

1875 The Bombay Stock Exchange in India is established, becoming the first stockbrokers' association in Asia.

1875 A pre-Columbian Chac Mool sculpture is excavated from the Platform of the Eagles and Jaguars at Chichen Itza, Yucatán. It will later influence Henry Moore's sculpture style.

1875 The Ottoman state declares partial bankruptcy and places its finances in the hands of its European creditors.

1876 The Reichsbank opens in Berlin. It produces legal tender (the Goldmark) until 1914 when the link between the mark and gold is abandoned.

1876 Alexander Graham Bell invents the telephone and makes the first successful call saying, 'Mr. Watson, come here, I want to see you.'

1877 Edgar Degas paints *Dancers practising at the Barre*.

1877 Australia beats England in the first cricket Test match. The series becomes known as The Ashes.

1877 Tchaikovsky's ballet *Swan Lake* premières at the Bolshoi Theatre in Moscow.

1878 *Sallie Gardner at a Gallop*, the first motion picture, is recorded using 24 photographs in a fast-motion series that are shown on a zoopraxiscope.

1878 Friedrich Nietzsche publishes *Human, All Too Human: A Book for Free Spirits*.

1879 New York City's Gilmore's Garden is renamed Madison Square Garden by William Henry Vanderbilt, and is opened to the public.

1879 *A Doll's House* by Henrik Ibsen is published and premières in Copenhagen. For the play's German debut, Ibsen is forced to write an alternative ending in keeping with traditional expectations as to how a wife and mother would act.

1880 Greenwich Mean Time is legally adopted in Britain.

1881 The world's oldest international sport federation, *Federation Internationale de Gymnastique,* is founded.

1882 Ferdinand von Lindeman proves that π is transcendental.

1882 Heinrich Koch isolates *Tuberculosis bacillus*.

1883 *The Adventures of Pinocchio* by Carlo Collodi is published.

1883 The quagga - half zebra, half horse - once very common in South Africa, becomes extinct.

1884 Anton Chekhov qualifies as a physician although he makes little money from the profession and treats the poor for free.

1884 The Hungarian Royal Opera House in Budapest opens to the public.

1884 Georges Seurat begins to paint *A Sunday Afternoon on the Island of La Grande Jatte,* the first painting in the pointillist style initiating Neo-impressionism.

1885 Nicola Tesla redesigns Edison's inefficient motor and generators based on a promise (he claims Edison made) of $50,000. Tesla inquires about payment and Edison replies, 'Tesla, you don't understand our American humor' and offers him an increase in salary from $18 a week to $28. Tesla immediately resigns.

1885 Carl Fabergé makes his first jewelled egg for Tsar Alexander III of Russia.

c1885 Berthe Morisot paints *Girl on a Divan*.

1885 The rollercoaster is patented.

1886 The first official world Chess Championship is held with Wilhelm Steinitz beating the Polish-born master Johannes Zukertort.

1886 The world's first motor car, the Benz Patent Motorwagen, is unveiled by Karl Benz.

1887 The Michelson and Morley experiments refute the ether theory.

1887 The first All-Ireland Football and Hurling Championships are played.

1888 Hertz demonstrates radio waves, a part of the electromagnetic spectrum.

1888 Stanislavski takes the role of the Knight in a production of Alexander Pushkin's *The Miserly Knight*.

1888 Thomas Edison holds a press conference to demonstrate his gramophone, playing one of the first recordings of music ever made.

1888 Vincent van Gogh paints *The Sunflowers*. He associated yellow with hope and friendship saying it was 'an idea expressing gratitude'. He hangs the painting in the guest bedroom in Arles in anticipation of the arrival of his friend Gauguin.

1889 The Eiffel Tower is completed. Seventy-two names of French scientists, engineers and notables are engraved on the structure but no women are included in the list.

1890 Tsar Alexander III of Russia establishes the Trans-Siberian Railway.

1890 The first known crossword puzzle appears in the Italian magazine *Il Secolo Illustrato*.

1891 Basketball is invented by James Naismith in the USA.
1891 Oscar Wilde's *The Soul of Man under Socialism* is published.
1892 The Ellis Island immigrant station officially opens on 1st January. A 14 year-old Irish girl, Annie Moore, is the first passenger to register.
1893 New Zealand becomes the first country to give women the right to vote in national elections.
1893 At the Chicago World Fair, Nikola Tesla lights a wireless gas-discharge lamp using a high-voltage high-frequency alternating current.
1893 Maria Montessori enters the medical program at the University of Rome. Her attendance at classes with men in the presence of a naked body is deemed inappropriate and she is required to perform her dissections of cadavers alone, after hours.
1894 Anton Chekhov begins writing *The Seagull* in a lodge in the orchard of his small estate in Melikhovo, a town 40 miles south of Moscow.
1894 Alexandre Yersin isolates the bacterium that caused the third pandemic of the bubonic plague.
1894 Ireland wins the Rugby Triple Crown for the first time.
1894 *The Time Machine* by H G Wells is published.
1895 The first Venice Biennale is held.
1895 The London School of Economics is co-founded by George Bernard Shaw.
1895 Ivan Pavlov analyzes the saliva and response of dogs to food under different conditions.
1895 Wilhelm Röntgen discovers X-rays.
1895 *The Importance of Being Earnest, A Trivial Comedy for Serious People* by Oscar Wilde is first performed at the St James's Theatre in London.
1896 The first modern Olympic games are held in Athens.
1897 *Dracula* by Bram Stoker is published.
1897 Aspirin (acetylsalicylic acid) is first isolated by Felix Hoffmann in Germany.
1897 Guglielmo Marconi sends the first wireless communication over open sea.
1898 Joshua Slocum completes the first single-handed circumnavigation of the world in *The Spray* (11.2m).
1898 Radium is discovered by Marie Skłodowska-Curie and her husband Pierre in a uraninite sample. Ernest Rutherford identifies alpha and beta particles.
1900 *The Wonderful Wizard of Oz* by L Frank Baum is published.
c1900 Paul Cézanne paints *The Bathers*.
1900 Karl Landsteiner identifies the main blood groups.
1900 Max Planck postulates that electromagnetic energy can only be emitted in quantized form – the birth of quantum physics.
1900 The Antikythera mechanism, an ancient device used to calculate astronomical positions, is recovered from a wreck in the Aegean Sea.
1901 A semiconductor crystal rectifier for detecting radio waves, described as Cat's Whiskers, is patented by Chandra Bose.
1902 Flirting in public is outlawed in New York State.
1902 Auguste Rodin sculpts *The Thinker*.
1902 Irish born Mary Harris, later known as Mother Jones, is considered to be the 'most dangerous woman in America' due to her militancy with the labour unions.
1902 Gustav Klimt creates the *Beethoven Frieze* for the Viennese Secession Building.
1903 The first Tour de France is held to increase paper sales for the magazine *L'Auto* (*L'Équipe*).
1903 The Wright brothers build and fly the first successful aeroplane at Kittyhawk, North Carolina.
1903 Edwin S. Porter's film *The Great Train Robbery* starring Broncho Billy Anderson, is released.
1904 James Joyce has his first outing with Nora Barnacle in Dublin on June 16th, the date on which his novel Ulysses is based, now celebrated as Bloomsday.
1905 'Sensible and responsible women do not want to vote' states Grover Cleveland, U.S. President.

1905 Albert Einstein proposes the law of the photoelectric effect and special relativity $E=mc^2$ – his 'Miraculous Year'.
1905 A dimple pattern is applied to golf balls maximising lift and minimising drag.
1905 Sigmund Freud's Three Essays on the *Theory of Sexuality and Jokes and their Relation to the Unconscious* is published.
1905 Tsar Nicholas II agrees to a constitution, devolution of some power to the Duma, and a free press.
1907 The Suffragettes march through London, led by Emily Pankhurst.
1907 George Soper identifies Mary Mallon as an asymptomatic carrier of typhoid in New York – Typhoid Mary.
1907 The first *Casa dei Bambini* (Children's House) overseen by Maria Montessori opens in Rome.
1908 Kristian Birkeland proposes that the Aurora borealis phenomenon is connected to geomagnetic field lines.
1909 Lansteiner, Levaditi and Popper discover the polio virus.
1909 Pablo Picasso and Georges Braque invent *Analytic Cubism*.
1910 The Casa Milà is constructed in Barcelona.
1911 *Alexander's Ragtime Band* by Irving Berlin becomes a major hit.
1911 Roald Amundsen and his team reach the South Pole.
1912 Photo finish is used for the first time at the Summer Olympics in Stockholm.
1912 A German archaeological team discovers the Nefertiti bust in Thutmose's workshop in Amarna, Egypt.
1912 The Russian Social Democratic Labour Party, under the leadership of Vladimir Lenin decides to make *Pravda* its official mouthpiece.
1912 RMS *Titanic* departs on her maiden voyage from Cork, Ireland.
1913 The premiere of Stravinsky's *Rite of Spring* is presented as a ballet, choreographed by Vaslav Nijinsky, in Paris. The avant-garde nature of the music and choreography causes a near-riot in the audience.
1913 Marcel Proust pays for publication of the first volume of *À la Recherche du Temps Perdu*.
1913 Neils Bohr proposes the quantum theory of atomic orbits.
1913 Henry Ford installs the first modern assembly line for motor cars.
1914 On Christmas Eve during World War 1, British and German soldiers climb out from the trenches into 'no man's land' and sing carols while sharing cake and cigars. A spontaneous truce extends for hundreds of miles amongst thousands of soldiers.
1914 The Panama Canal opens.
1915 Ernest Shackleton and his trans-Antarctic Expedition team spend the polar winter on their ship *Endurance* as it is slowly crushed by ice in the Weddell Sea, on the coast of Antarctica.
1915 Einstein proposes the General Theory of Relativity.
1916 Margaret Sanger opens the first birth control clinic in the United States, leading to her arrest for distributing information on contraception.
1916 The Easter Rising in Ireland. The Battle of the Somme in France.
1916 Shackleton and five crew members depart from Elephant Island in a small open boat on a rescue mission. They reach the uninhabited southern coast of South Georgia 15 days later having survived an 800 nautical mile trip on the southern ocean.
1916 Giorgio de Chirico paints *The Disquieting Muses* inspiring Sylvia Plath's poem of the same title, written in 1957.
1916 *Dadaism*, an art movement of the European avant-garde, begins in Zurich, Switzerland.
1918 Countess Markievicz is the first woman to be elected to the British House of Commons.
1918 Reconstruction begins on the *Prambanan*, a 9th-century Hindu temple compound in Central Java.
1919 *Desert Gold*, a New Zealand thoroughbred racehorse, wins her 19th race in succession.
1919 Aurthur Eddington observes gravity bending starlight during a solar eclipse - the first supporting evidence for Einstein's General Relativity prediction.
c1920 Irish architect Eileen Gray designs the Bibendum Chair.
1920 Mustafa Kemal Atatürk becomes president of Turkey.
c1920 Coco Chanel designs what will become known as the 'little black dress'.

1920   Prohibition is enforced in the United States.

1922   *Ulysses* by James Joyce is published by Sylvia Beach, in Paris.

1922   Frederick Banting and Charles Best discover insulin.

1922   The Irish Free State is formed.

1922   The tomb of *Tutankhamun* is discovered in Egypt.

1923   The 24 Hours of Le Mans sports car race is held for the first time.

1923   Ernest Hemmingway takes up bull fighting and big game hunting in Spain.

1924   Louis de Broglie proposes the theory that matter has a wave-like nature.

1924   The first winter Olympic games are held in Chamonix, France.

1924   George Gershwin composes *Rhapsody in Blue*.

1925   Herbert Bayer develops the designs for universal lettering for the Bauhaus letterhead.

1925   John Logie Baird successfully transmits the first televised silhouette images in motion – television.

1925   *The Great Gatsby* by F Scott Fitzgerald is published.

1926   Robert Goddard builds and launches the world's first liquid-fuelled rocket.

1927   Mies van der Rohe designs the German Pavilion for the International Exposition in Barcelona.

1927   *The Jazz Singer* starring Al Jolson is the first feature length 'talkie' film released.

1927   The first World Snooker Championship is played in Birmingham, England.

1927   *To the Lighthouse* by Virginia Woolf is published.

1928   Alexander Fleming discovers the antibiotic effect of Penicillin.

1928   Paul Dirac predicts the existence of antimatter.

1929   The excavation of Petra in Jordan.

1929   Herge's *Tintin* first appears.

1929   The Graf Zeppelin becomes the first airship to circumnavigate the world.

1929   Shostakovich composes the film score for the silent movie *The New Babylon*, set during the 1871 Paris Commune.

1930   Mahatma Gandhi leads a march from Ahmedabad to the coast of India and picks up salt in defiance of the salt tax, triggering the non-violent civil disobedience movement in India.

1930   Uruguay hosts and wins the first soccer World Cup.

1930   The first dive in a bathysphere is made by by Otis Barton and Charles Beebe. They descend to a depth of 183m.

1931   The Empire State building opens.

1931   *Histoire de Babar* by Jean de Brunhoff is published

1932   John Cockcroft and Ernest Walton split the atom using a particle accelerator.

1932   Alvar Aalto designs a new form of laminated bent-plywood furniture.

1932   Amelia Earhart is the first woman to fly solo across the Atlantic - from Newfoundland to Derry in Northern Ireland.

1933   The first American comic book is published *Famous Funnies: A Carnival of Comics*.

1933   John Desmond Bernal investigates the structure of liquid water and discovers the boomerang shape of its H_2O molecule.

1934   Sergei Rachmaninoff composes *Rhapsody on a Theme of Paganini*.

1935   Nylon is first synthesised.

1935   Schrödinger's Cat thought experiment is proposed.

1935   The first paperback *Penguin Books* are published.

1935   Radar systems are developed in secrecy by up to thirteen countries including the United States, Great Britain, Germany, the USSR, Japan, the Netherlands, France and Italy.

1936   Gynmastics for women is added to the Olympic program at the Berlin Games.

1937   Journalist Martha Gellhorn travels to Spain to cover the civil war.

1937   Pablo Picasso paints *Guernica*.

1937   Disney releases *Snow White*, the first full-colour animated film.

1938   Freda Kahlo paints the first of her *Self-portraits with a Monkey*.

1938   The DC Comics hero *Superman* first appears.

1939   Salvador Dalí paints *Shirley Temple, the Youngest Sacred Monster of Contemporary Cinema*.

1939   Judy Garland stars in *The Wizard of Oz*.

1939   Bertolt Brecht writes *Mother Courage and Her Children* with significant contributions by Margarete Steffin.

1939   Alan Turing's electromechanical machine (the Bombe) deciphers the Enigma codes.

1940   The first metallic hip replacement surgery is performed at Johns Hopkins Hospital, USA. Twenty years later the use of ivory prostheses is pioneered in Mandalay, Burma.

1940   Upper Paleolithic art 17,300 years old is discovered in the Lascaux Cave in the Dordogne, France.

1941   Billy Strayhorn's *Take the 'A' Train* is recorded and becomes the signature tune of the Duke Ellington Orchestra. The title refers to the new subway running from eastern Brooklyn into Harlem.

1941   *Dumbo* is produced by Walt Disney.

1941   Orson Welles directs and stars in Citizen Kane.

1941   A special Monopoly edition is created for World War II prisoners of war. Hidden inside are items such as maps and compasses to aid escapes.

1942   Edward Hopper paints *Nighthawks*.

1942   *L'Étranger* (The Outsider) by Albert Camus is published.

1942   Enrico Fermi achieves the first self-sustaining fission chain reaction.

1944   The International Monetary Fund (IMF) and the World Bank are founded.

1945   The concentration camp at Auschwitz is liberated by Soviet troops on 27th January, now Holocaust Memorial Day.

1945   The 'Trinity' test, the first detonation of a nuclear weapon, takes place in the New Mexico desert on 16th July.

1946   Colonel Juan Perón is elected president of Argentina and his wife, Eva Perón (Evita), is put in charge of labour relations.

1946   Piaggio designs the Vespa scooter.

1946   Parker Brothers brings out *Game of Rich Uncle* featuring Rich Uncle Pennybags.

1946   Soviet school children present a wooden replica of the Great Seal of the United States to the US Ambassador at the Moscow embassy. In 1952 it is discovered that the seal contains a microphone.

1947   *The Annex: Diary Notes from 14 June 1942 – 1 August 1944* is published in Amsterdam and later translated as *Anne Frank: The Diary of a Young Girl*.

1947   India becomes an independent state under Prime Minister Pandit Nehru.

1949   1984 by George Orwell is published.

1949   *Le Deuxième Sexe* by Simone de Beauvoir is published.

1949   The Carbon-14 isotope is first used for radiocarbon dating of archaeological and geological samples.

1949   The first atomic clock is constructed.

1950   *I, Robot* a collection of nine stories by Isaac Asimov is published.

1950   Polio vaccines are developed independently by Koprowski, Salk and Sabin. In 1962 Sabin's live vaccine (Oral Polio Vaccine) is adopted worldwide.

1951   *The Catcher in the Rye* by J D Salinger is published.

1952   In Helsinki, Czechoslovakian Emil Zátopek sets Olympic records in the 5,000m, 10,000m, and the marathon in which he had never run before.

1952   *Galatea of the Spheres* is painted by Salvador Dalí.

1952   *The Old Man and the Sea* by Ernest Hemmingway is published.

1952   Rosalind Franklin produces X-ray diffraction images of DNA.

1953   James Watson and Francis Crick discover the double helix structure for DNA.

1953   *En attendant Godot* (Waiting for Godot) by Samuel Beckett, premières in the Théâtre de Babylone in Paris.

1953   Edmund Hillary and Tenzing Norgay reach the summit of Mount Everest.

1953   M C Escher creates the lithograph *Relativity*.

1954   The first silicon transistor is fabricated at Bell Labs.

1954   The first organ transplant (a kidney) is performed.

1955   In Alabama, Rosa Parks refuses to obey a bus driver's order to give up her seat for a white passenger.

| 1955 | Einstein and Bertrand Russell sign a manifesto highlighting the danger posed by nuclear weapons. Three years later Linus Pauling presents the United Nations with a petition signed by more than 11,000 scientists calling for an end to nuclear weapon testing. |

1955 Einstein and Bertrand Russell sign a manifesto highlighting the danger posed by nuclear weapons. Three years later Linus Pauling presents the United Nations with a petition signed by more than 11,000 scientists calling for an end to nuclear weapon testing.

1957 *That'll be the day* by Buddy Holly is released.

1957 Pelé makes his debut with Santos and Brazil wins the World Cup the following year.

1957 The space race begins with Sputnik 1 launched into an elliptical low Earth orbit.

1958 The first integrated circuits – the basis of all modern computer chips – are fabricated.

1958 *Things Fall Apart* by Nigerian Chinua Achebe is published. The title is taken from a line in a W B Yeats poem: *Things fall apart; the centre cannot hold;*

1959 Richard Feynman proposes the possibility of nano-scale machines.

1959 The Guggenheim Museum, designed by Frank Lloyd Wright opens in New York.

1960 *To Kill a Mockingbird* by Harper Lee is published.

1960 In Sri Lanka, Sirimavo Bandaranaike becomes the world's first female prime minister.

1960 Harry Ferguson designs the world's first 4 wheel-drive Formula 1 car in which Stirling Moss wins the Gold Cup the following year.

1960 Pulses of light are produced from a pink-ruby crystal – the laser is born.

1960 In Rome, 400 athletes from 23 countries compete in the Parallel Olympics, the first Paralympics.

1960 *La Dolce Vita* directed by Federico Fellini is released.

1961 Cosmonaut Yuri Gagarin is the first human to journey into outer space, when his Vostok spacecraft completes an orbit of the Earth on 12 April in 1961.

1962 *Silent Spring* by Rachel Carson is published.

1962 Andy Warhol creates the silkscreen *Marilyn Diptych*.

1962 *A Clockwork Orange* by Anthony Burgess is published.

1962 The Beatles first single, *Love Me Do*, is released.

1962 *Dr No*, the first Bond film is released.

1963 Edward Lorenz publishes his discovery of the 'butterfly effect', significant in the development of chaos theory.

1963 'I have a Dream' - Martin Luther King speaks from the steps of the Lincoln Memorial.

1965 Mao Zedong starts the Cultural Revolution in China.

1966 Dr Christiaan Barnard performs the first successful human-to-human heart transplant in Cape Town, South Africa, on a man who survives for eighteen days.

1966 Indira Ghandi becomes Prime Minister of India, one of the first women elected to lead a nation.

1966 Seamus Heaney's first full-length collection of poetry *Death of a Naturalist* is published.

1967 Procol Harum's debut song *A Whiter Shade of Pale*, based on the Bach melody Air on a G String (1720), becomes one of the anthems of the Summer of Love in Haight-Ashbury, San Francisco.

1967 Argentinian Marxist revolutionary Che Guevara is executed in Bolivia.

1967 Pulsars, rotating neutron stars, are first detected.

1967 *The Third Policeman* by Brian O'Nolan is published posthumously under the pseudonym Flann O'Brien.

1968 *2001: A Space Odyssey* directed by Stanley Kubrick is released.

1969 Neil Armstrong is the first man to walk on the moon.

1969 Woodstock music festival is held at a dairy farm in the Catskills near the town of Bethel, New York.

1970 The Trans-Amazonian Highway project encourages settlement in the Amazon rainforest but many native species are put in danger.

1970 Kraftwerk Electronic Music Project is formed by Ralf Hütter and Florian Schneider.

1970 The Caspian tiger becomes extinct.

1970 The World Series of poker begins in Las Vegas.

1971 In Switzerland women are given the right to vote in federal elections and stand for parliament for the first time.

1972 The first patent for an MRI machine is issued.

1972 *The Magnavox Odyssey* is released - the first home video game console that can be connected to a TV set.

1972 Lou Reed's song *Walk on the Wild Side* is included in his second solo album *Transformer.*

1973 The first call is made on a hand held mobile phone (in a non-vehicle setting) using microwave technology.

1973 Alexandr Solzhenitsyn's *The Gulag Archipelago,* based on his experiences in a Soviet forced labour camp, is published in the West.

1973 The Sydney Opera House is completed.

1974 The first transgenic mammal is created by integrating DNA from the SV40 virus into the genome of mice.

1974 The Terracotta Army is discovered near the Mausoleum of the First Qín Emperor.

1975 Borobudur, a 9th-century Mahayana Buddhist Temple in Indonesia, is restored.

1975 *Bohemian Rhapsody* is recorded by Queen.

1975 Mandlebrot introduces the term 'fractal'.

1975 *The Periodic Table* by Primo Levi is published.

1977 Organisms whose life is based on chemosynthesis, rather than photosynthesis, are discovered living around the deep sea vents of the Galápagos Islands.

1977 The first photograph of the Earth and moon together in space is taken by the *Voyager 1* probe.

1977 Wangari Maathai establishes the *Green Belt Movement* in Kenya. She becomes the first African woman to receive the Nobel Peace Prize in 2004.

1977 Smallpox is eradicated due to vaccination.

1978 Polish woman, Chojnowska-Liskiewicz, is the first woman to sail single-handed around the world.

1978 The first successful human birth as a result of in-vitro fertilisation.

1978 Volkswagen manufactures its last Beetle.

1978 The Rock-Hewn Churches, Lalibela, in Ethiopia are listed as a UNESCO World Heritage Site.

1981 A man working on a malfunctioning robot at a car manufacturing plant in Japan is killed when the robot's arm pushes him into a grinding machine.

1981 *Shergar* wins the Epsom Derby by a record 10 lengths, the longest winning margin in the race's 226-year history. Two years later Shergar is kidnapped but the body is never recovered.

1981 Superstring theory is first proposed.

1982 The Internet protocol suite (TCP/IP) is standardised enabling the concept of a world-wide network to develop.

1982 Elk Cloner is one of the first known microcomputer viruses to spread 'in the wild' via floppy disc.

1982 The film *Blade Runner* based on Philip K Dick's novel *Do Androids Dream of Electric Sheep?* is released.

1984 The first TED conference is launched to brainstorm the powerful convergence between Technology, Entertainment and Design.

1984 *L'Insoutenable légèreté de l'être* (The Unbearable Lightness of Being) by Milan Kundera is first published in a French translation. The original Czech text is published the following year.

1985 A hole in the ozone layer over Antarctica is identified.

1985 Andy Warhol creates the *Reigning Queen* series – portraits of the queens of Denmark, Swaziland, the Netherlands and Britain.

1985 Buckminsterfullerene, a spherical allotrope of carbon, is discovered.

1985 The Australian government returns ownership of *Uluru* (Ayres Rock) to the local Pitjantjatjara Aboriginal people.

1986 Maradona scores the 'Hand of God' goal during the 2–1 victory for Argentina over England in the quarter final of the World Cup.

1986 *Graceland* by Paul Simon featuring Ladysmith Black Mambazo is released.

1986	Nigerian Wole Soyinka becomes the first person from the continent of Africa to receive the Nobel Prize in literature.
1987	Gödel's ontological proof of the existence of God is published posthumously.
1987	The 'Mitochondrial Eve' hypothesis is proposed: all living humans are descended from one woman.
1987	A high-speed train system in Japan is based on the mathematics of fuzzy logic.
1988	The Morris Worm is released on the Internet and results in the first conviction in the US under the Computer Fraud and Abuse Act.
1988	Nora: The real Life of Molly Bloom by Brenda Maddox is published.
1988	Table tennis becomes an Olympic sport.
1989	The first episode of The Simpsons is broadcast.
1989	The Berlin Wall comes down.
1990	Nelson Mandela is freed from prison after serving 27 years.
1990	A team of divers off the coast of Alexandria discover stone blocks from the Pharos Lighthouse, one of the lost Seven Wonders of the ancient world. They also find the submerged ruins of Cleopatra's palace and temple complex.
1990	The first dog sled crossing of Antarctica is completed.
1990	Hubble, the first optical based space telescope, is launched into orbit.
1991	The World Wide Web is launched at CERN.
1991	The Pretty Good Privacy (PGP) data encryption program is written and becomes the first widely available program implementing public-key cryptography.
1992	More than 100 world leaders meet in Rio de Janeiro for the first international Earth Summit.
1992	The cosmic microwave background is observed, supporting Lemaître's Big Bang Theory of 1929.
1994	Knowledge of Angels by Jill Paton Walsh is published. The plot is based on a true story about a feral woman found in France in 1731, the Maid of Châlons.
1994	South Africa holds its first universal elections and Nelson Mandela is inaugurated as president. South Africa wins the Rugby World Cup the following year.
1995	Marie Curie becomes the first woman to be entombed on her own merit in the Panthéon in Paris.
1995	Longitude by Dava Sobel is published.
1995	Wolves are reintroduced to Yellowstone National Park.
1995	Barings Bank, the oldest merchant bank in London, collapses.
1996	Dolly the sheep, the first mammal to be cloned from an adult cell, is born.
1997	China regains control of Hong Kong after 99 years of British rule.
1997	Deep Blue, a chess-playing computer, wins a six-game match against world champion Garry Kasparov.
1997	Quantum bit (qubit) teleportation is demonstrated at Innsbruck, Austria.
1997	The Guggenheim Museum in Bilbao is completed.
1998	A 40-million-year-old preserved lizard is found in a lump of amber in Gdansk, Poland.
1998	The play Copenhagen by Michael Frayn debuts in London. The plot is based on a meeting that took place between Danish atomic physicist Niels Bohr and German theoretical physicist Werner Heisenberg in 1941.
1998	The bacterium thiomargarita namibiensis is found off the coast of Namibia. It has cells large enough (max 0.75mm) to be visible to the naked eye.
1999	E-mail systems across the world become congested due to propagation of the Melissa virus.
1999	Cueva de las Manos (Cave of Hands) in Argentina is listed as a UNESCO World Heritage Site. The age of the paintings (c7350 BC) is dated from the remains of the bone-made pipes used for spraying the 'paint' on the rock walls to create silhouettes of hands.
1999	Nunavut in Canada becomes a self-governing Inuit territory.

2000 – 2010	During the first decade of the third millennium Argentina, Brazil, Chile, Costa Rica, Finland, India, Indonesia, Liberia, Lithuania and South Korea each elect their first female president. The United States elects its first African-American president.
2000	Pope John Paul II issues a formal apology on behalf of the Catholic Church for the trial of Galileo.
2001	Wikipedia, an open source online encyclopedia, is launched.
2002	The Bibliotheca Alexandrina opens in Alexandria, a library with room for up to five million books. It is built to pay tribute to the ancient library that stood in Alexandria during the Ptolemaic dynasty, almost 2,500 years previously.
2003	Clonycavan Man, an Iron Age bog body, is found in County Meath, Ireland.
2003	Complete expression of the human genome is revealed.
2005	Salvator Mundi, the sixteenth painting accredited to Leonardo da Vinci, is rediscovered.
2005	Surgeons in France carry out the first human face transplant.
2007	Electron tunnelling using an attosecond laser pulse is observed.
2010	Chinese artist Ai Weiwei exhibits more than 100 million handmade porcelain sunflower seeds at the Tate modern in London.
2010	Aung San Suu Kyi is released from house arrest in Burma.
2010	The world's tallest man-made structure, the 829.8m Burj Khalifa in Dubai, United Arab Emirates is completed.
2010	Antimatter is successfully trapped for the first time, with 38 antihydrogen atoms held in place for a fraction of a second.
2010	The sculpture L'Homme qui marche I created by Alberto Giacometti in 1961 is auctioned for £65 million.
2010	The first 24-hour flight by a solar-powered plane is completed.
2011	The population of the world passes seven billion.
2012	Researchers successfully perform the first implantation of an early prototype bionic eye.
2012	Lonesome George dies - the last known of this subspecies of Galápagos tortoise.
2012	The rover Curiosity lands on Mars.
2012	The Higgs boson is detected at CERN.
2013	The Voyager probe, launched in 1977, reaches almost 19 billion kilometres from Earth and becomes the first man made object to leave the solar system.
2013	Human embryonic cells are first created by cloning.
2013	The concentration of carbon dioxide in the atmosphere exceeds 400 parts per million.

ACKNOWLEDGEMENTS

Working for the Institute of Physics as their representative in Ireland for almost thirteen years provided me with fertile ground to develop my interest in outreach. I thank everyone I worked with there, in particular the officers, committee members and many volunteers who were all so supportive and engaged. It was a joy to work with my friend and colleague, Sheila Gilheany, for so many years and it is apposite that the last major outreach project we worked on together was the Physics in Time Poster - the stepping-stone for this project.

I was introduced to Tony Scott, the co-founder of the Young Scientist in Ireland, when I started working for the Institute of Physics at the turn of the millennium, and we shared an office for many years. Tony's friendship and support, both professional and personal, has been a wonderful constant in my life. No finer person could have launched this book.

I first met Garrett Bennis and Daniel Morehead of Origin Design when working on the Physics in Time project. This was one of those lucky moments when I sensed that Origin had an energy and passion that matched my own - to produce an innovative, beautiful yet educational resource. Sarah Moloney, a young designer/illustrator, joined Origin in January 2013. When I first saw Sarah's brilliant illustrations I knew the design was going to be very special. Origin's ability to understand the brief and create original concepts from the lists of facts was remarkable - this was a super team to work with, in every way.

The journey to distill the essence of The Visual Time Traveller had many pivotal moments but time and time again Garrett had an intuitive feeling for the right direction to take. His skill in Art Direction meant not only that my dreams were realised, but were improved! Garrett's belief in the project (and support for me) has been integral to its success. I am indebted to him.

Iliana Chatzifragkou provided the Greek translation on the Rosetta stone spread (1820-1825) and Ahmed abu-Shanab provided the Arabic translation. These translations were done with such efficiency and generosity – I am very grateful to them both. Thank you to Julianna Szabo who won the student competition with her clever design concept for 1770 – 1775, which we adapted for the book.

Photograph, Bryan James Brophy

Alison was born in Cork and educated at Trinity College Dublin, graduating in Mathematics and Economics in 1982. She is the founder of 21st Century Renaissance, a movement dedicated to using original design combined with writing to influence change and raise debate across a wide section of society. Her belief is that an educational system must enable young people to become compassionate, clear, imaginative thinkers and life long learners. She lives in Dún Laoghaire close to the sea, but not quite as close as her first home in Currabinny, on the south coast of Ireland.

I thank Eleanor Collier for her careful and thoughtful editing and proofing - not an easy task once the text was integrated into the designs - her advice was invaluable, every time.

John Montayne's advice regarding the online presence for the project was invaluable and offered with a great injection of encouragement at just the right time. Suzanne Fogarty and Stephen Cahill provided probably the most important bit of all – financial advice. My sincere thanks to them both for keeping me on the straight and narrow!

The Royal Dublin Society provided me not only with a second home, but critical support and advice at the latter stages of the project. My particular thanks to librarian Gerard Whelan for his help on a number of fronts.

My thanks to the following (in no particular order) for their guidance or support, in one way or another, on this extraordinary journey - Kingsley Aikins, Mary Apied, David Brennan, Carey Clarke, Rebecca Gale, Gerry Gardner, Patrick Gleeson, Shayne Hallahan, John Kealy, Pauline Logan, Paul McGrath, Fonsie Mealy, Niamh Morris, Elizabeth Muller, Patrick Murphy, Owen O'Doherty, John O'Hagan, Gina Quin, Pauline Scott and Arlene Sommerville.

Support from my extended family and friends was invaluable during this all-consuming project (too many for me to mention, but you know who you are). I thank you all for enduring my somewhat obsessive and compulsive nature since the Autumn of 2012 when you had to listen, whether you wanted to or not! Furthermore, during a very difficult time for me personally, at the beginning of this year, your gentle arms (both literal and metaphorical) were around my shoulders – shelter during a storm.

The virtual side of The Visual Time Traveller (and moral backup) was aided and abetted by my grown up children who I adore - Aisling, David and Nicholas.

For Justin, words are inadequate, but I'll try. You are wise, kind and always there.
Thank you, from the heart.